# Hand Book of Microbiology & Parasitology

**U.N. PANDA**
MD, CMO (SG), New Delhi

**AITBS PUBLISHERS, INDIA**
MEDICAL PUBLISHERS
J-5/6, Krishan Nagar, Delhi-110051 (INDIA)
Phone: 011-40167052, 49067602
E-mail: aitbsindia@gmail.com & aitbsindia@hotmail.com

First Edition : 2005
Second Edition : 2016
Third Edition : 2026

ISBN: 978-93-7473-289-7

*Published by:*
Virender Kumar Arya for
**AITBS Publishers, India**
**MEDICAL PUBLISHERS**
J-5/6, Krishan Nagar, Delhi-110051 (INDIA)
Phone: 011-40167052, 49067602
E-mail: aitbsindia@gmail.com & aitbsindia@hotmail.com

Printed by AITBS, Delhi

# *Preface*

Most human diseases are caused by micro organisms, either by their direct cytopathic effect or by immune aberration. In developing and under developed countries parasites and helminths claim many lives. Hence study of microbiology and parasitology is of immense importance for medical as well as dental students; students of physiotherapy and nursing and all personnel involved in health care delivery.

In this small handbook I have tried to depict the voluminous texts of microbiology and parasitology in a crisp and concise manner. Detailed descriptions have been deliberately omitted. I am sure the book will be of immense help to students of medicine, dentistry, physiotherapy, nursing and allied health care personnel. All suggestions for improvement are cordially welcome.

*U.N. Panda*

# CONTENTS

# 1

# *Introduction to Microbiology*

*Microbiology* is the study of living organisms of microscopic size, which includes bacteria, fungi, algae, protozoa and the viruses. It is concerned with their form, structure, reproduction, physiology, metabolism and classification. Most micro organisms are unicellular. Regardless of the complexity of an organism, the cell is the structural unit of life. All living cells are fundamentally similar. The word cell was coined by Robert Hooke in 1685. Cell can be eucaryotic or procaryotic (See below Table 1.1).

**Table 1.1 Features distinguishing procaryotic from eucaryotic cells**

| *Features* | *Procaryotic cell* | *Eucaryotic cell* |
|---|---|---|
| | Bacteria | Algae, fungi, proto zoa, plant, animal |
| Size | 1-4μ | 5μ and more |
| Nucleus | Not bounded by nuclear membrane, one circular chromosome | Bounded by nuclear membrane, more than one chromosome |
| Nucleolus | Absent | Present |
| Cytoplasmic streaming | Absent | Present |
| Mesosomes | Present | Absent |
| Ribosomes | 70 S in cytoplasm | 80 S in endoplasmic reticulum, 70 S in mitochondria |
| Mitochondria | Absent | Present |

| | | |
|---|---|---|
| Golgi apparatus | Absent | Present |
| Endoplasmic reticulum | Absent | Present |
| Cell wall | Peptidoglycan present but sterols absent | Peptidoglycan absent but sterols present. |
| Metabolzen | Often araerobic, some fix nitrogen and some accumulate poly β hydroxybutyrate | Glycolytic |

## The Characterization, Classification and Identification of Microorganisms

Classification is a means of bringing order to bewildering variety of organisms in nature. The characteristic of microorganism must be known before it is classified. Characteristics are studied in culture. The major characteristics of microorganisms fall into the following categories.

1. Morphological characteristics : Cell size, shape and structure, cell arrangement pattern, staining property, motility and flagellar arrangement, occurrence of special structures and developmental forms.
2. Chemical composition
3. Cultural characteristics : Nutrition requirement and physical conditions required for growth, and the manner in which growth occurs.
4. Metabiotic characteristics : The way in which microorganism obtains, utilizes and stores energy, carries out metabolic reactions and regulates them.
5. Antigenic characteristics
6. Genetic characteristics : Characteristic of the cell

DNA and occurrences and function of other kinds of DNA that may be present, eg. plasmid.

7. Pathogenicity : Ability of organism to produce disease in plants, animals and other micro organisms.
8. Echological characteristics : Habitat and distribution of organism in nature and the interactions between and among species in natural environment.

Lipopolysaccharide in cell wall characterizes gram negative bacteria; gram position bacteria on the other hand have techoic acid in the cell wall.

Some microorganism grow in a medium only containing inorganic compounds while other require organic compounds like aminoacids, sugars, vitamins, coenzymes purines and pyrimidines. Some require complex natural substances like serum and blood or peptone, yeast autolysate. As yet some can not be grown on artificial media and require living cells or living hosts eg. chick embryo, mammalian tissue culture. In addition to specific nutrients, each kind of organism also requires specific physical conditions for growth e.g.; some bacteria only grow at temperature above 40°C while others grow best when temperature is below 20°C. Most bacteria pathogenic to humans require temperature close to that of human body (i.e., 37°C). Some bacteria are aerobic i.e., grow best in presence of $O_2$ while others are anaerobic. Cyanobacteria require light for their growth. On solid media microbes grow as colonies that have specific size, shape, colour, texture etc. Some bacteria oxidize various organic or inorganic compounds to obtain energy. While others obtain energy by redistributing the atoms within certain molecules. Antigenic characteristics of bacteria very widely but it has great practical importance in identifying the bacteria with specific antisera.

The double stranded chromosomal DNA of each kind of micro organism has certain features that are constant and hence useful for its classification. The sequence of nucleotide bases in DNA and DNA base composition (mol % G+C) are useful for this purpose. Pathologenicity of bacteria vary widely. While some are pathogenic to man, animals and plants, others can cause disease in other microorganism e.g.; bdellovibrios are predatory on other bacteria and bacteriophages (virus) destroy bacteria they infect. The habitat of microorganism also varies. Microbial population of oral cavity differs from that of intestinal tract and vagina. Micro organisms seen in marine environment differ from those seen in fresh water. While some microorganisms are widely distributed in nature, others are restricted to particular environments.

## Taxonomy

The basic taxonomic group is the species - i.e. a collection of strains having similar characteristics. A genus is composed of similar species. The goals of classification are for stability and predictability. The three methods used for arranging into taxonomic groups are intuitive method, numerical taxonomy and genetic relatedness. Classifications based on genetic relatedness come the closest to achieving the taxonomic goals of stability and predictability. The international code of nomenclature of bacteria was developed with reference to the much earlier established international codes of zoological and botanical nomenclature.

## Microscopic Examination of Microorganism

The microscope is the basic instrument for bacteriological examination as it provides magnification. Microscope can be optical microscope and electron microscope depending upon the principle on which magnification is based. Light microscopy can be (1) sbright field (2) dark field (3) fluorescent (4) phase contrast microscopy. In bright field microscopy, the microscopic field is illuminated and micro organisms appears dark as they absorb some light but staining them with a dye greatly increases their light absorbing ability with greater contrast and colour differentiation. The resolving power is the major drawback but not magnification. In *Dark Field Microscopy* a dark background is created against which objects are brilliantly illuminated by use of a special kind of condenser. A microbe appears bright aganist dark background. It is particularly valuable for wet mount and hanging drop preparation. Many chemical substances absorb light of particular wave length and then emit a light of longer wave length. Such substances are called fluorescent. For *Fluorescent Microscope* organisms are stained with a fluorescent dye and then illuminated with a blue light allowing a green fluorescence of the organism. In *Immune Fluorescence* fluorescent dye is combined with antibodies against microorganism. *Phase Contrast Microscope* is based on the principle that light passing through one material to another of different refractive index and/or thickness undergoes change in phase. *Electron Microscopy* achieves very high magnification and resolution with the extremely short wave length of electron bean it employs. (of 0.05A$^{o}$)

**Table 1.2 : Comparison of different types of Microscopy**

| *Microscope type* | *Maximum magnification* | *Appearance of specimen* | *Application* |
|---|---|---|---|
| Bright field | 1000-2000 | Specimen / bacteria take colour of stain | For gross morphology of bacteria, yeast, algae, |

| | | | |
|---|---|---|---|
| | | | protozoa |
| Dark field | 1000-2000 | Appear bright or 'lighted' in dark back ground | Darting motility of spirochaetes |
| Fluorescence | 1000-2000 | Organism takes colour of fluorescent dye | Identification of the organism |
| Phase contrast | 1000-2000 | Varying degrees of darkness | Identification of cellular retails of yeast, algae, protozoa |
| Electron | 200000-400000 | Viewed on fluorescent screen | Identification of virus and ultra-structure of bacteria |

## Milestones in Microbiology

| | |
|---|---|
| Louis Pasteur (1822-1895) | Germ theory of disease, and immunization |
| Florence Nightingale (1820-1910) | Organised inhospital care, to minimise cross infection |
| Joseph Lister (1827-1912) | Developed aseptic technique |
| John Tyndall (1820-1893) | Developed fractional sterilization to kill spores |
| Roberct Koch (1843-1910) | Discovered causative agents of anthrax, and tuberculosis |
| Paul Ehrlich (1854-1915) | Father of modern concept of chemo therapy |

| | |
|---|---|
| Elie Metchnikoff (1845-1916) | Discovered phagocytosis |
| William Henry Welch (1850-1934) | Discovered relation of clostridia to gas gangrene |
| Walter Reed (1851-1902) | Discovered transmission of yellow fever in mosquito |
| Octava Gengou (1875-1957) | Discovered complement fixation reaction |
| August von Wasser mann | Discovered complement fixation test for syphilis |
| Frederick W. Twort (1877-1950) | Discovered bacteriophages |
| Howard T Ricketts RMS | Reported wood tick transmitted |

**Microbial discovery - Milestones**

| *Year* | *Disease* | *Agent* | *Discoverer* |
|---|---|---|---|
| 1870 | Anthrax | *Bacillus anthracis* | Koch |
| 1879 | Gonorrhoea | *Neisseria gonorrhoea* | Neisser |
| 1880 | Typhoid | *Salmonella typhi* | Eberth |
| 1880 | Malaria | Plasmodium species | Laveran |
| 1881 | Wound sepsis | Staphylococcus | Ogston |
| 1882 | Tuberculosis | Mycobacterium | Koch |
| 1882 | Glanders | *Pseudomonas mallei* | Loeffler |
| 1883 | Cholera | Vibrio cholerae | Koch |
| 1883 | Diphtheria | *Corynebacterium diphtheriae* | Loeffler |
| 1885 | Tetanus | *Clostridium tetani* | Nicolaier |
| 1886 | Lobar pneumonia | Pneumococci | Frankel |
| 1887 | Mcningitis | Meningococcus | Welchselbaum |
| 1889 | Chancroid | *Haemophilus ducreyi* | Ducrey |
| 1892 | Gas gangrene | *Clostridium perfringens* | Welch & Nuttal |
| 1894 | Plague | *Pasteurella pestis* | Yersin |

| | | | |
|---|---|---|---|
| 1896 | Botulism | *Clostridium botulinum* | Van ermengem |
| 1898 | Bacillary dysentery | Shigella | Shiga |
| 1905 | Syphilis | *Treponema pallidum* | Hoffman |
| 1906 | Whooping cough | *Bordotella pertussis* | Bordet & Gengou |

## Germ theory of disease

Even before Psteur had proved experimentally about bacteria as the causes of many diseases, Fracastoro had suggested that disease was caused by invisible organisms. The contagiousness of puerperal fever was profounded by Olover Wendell Holmes in 1842. Pasteur subsequently isolated the parasite of silk worm disease, anthrax in cattles and sheeps followed by Robert Koch who grew anthrax bacilli on culture and was able to infect healthy animals with them. These observations led to the establishment of *Koch's Postulate* that reads (1) a specific organism can be found in association with a given disease (2) The organism can be isolated and grown in culture (3) The culture will produce the disease if injected into the healthy animal (4) The organism can be recovered form the infected animal.

## Microbial Stains

A large number of dyes are available for staining micro organisms. These dyes can be triphenylmethane dyes, oxazinc dyes and thiazine dyes. Chemically these dyes can be acid, basic or neutral. The acid dye has negative ion, basic dye position. Acid dyes stain basic cell components and basic dyes stain acidic cell components. The coloration of bacteria by applying a single solution of stain to a fixed smear is termed *Simple Stains*. Staining procedures that make visible the differences between bacterial cells or parts of a bacterial cell are termed *Differential Staining*. Gram stain is a commonly employed different staining introduced in 1884. The reagents used are crystal violet, iodine solution, alcohol (decolourizing agent) and safranin. The Gram positive bacteria retain crystal violet while gram mgative bacteria take up safranin. This so because (1) cell wall of gram negative bacteria is thin and contains higher percentnge of lipid (2) peptidoglyean content of gram negative bacterial cell wall is low.

| *Staining technique* | *Applocation* |
| --- | --- |
| Acid fast stain | Distinguishes mycobacterium species |
| Endospore stain | Demonstrates spores |
| Capsule stain | Demonstrates capsule |
| Flagells stain | Demonstrates arrangement of flagella |
| Cytoplasmic stain | Identifies intracellular deposits of starch, glycogen, poly phosphates |
| Giemsa stain | Stains rickettsia and some protozoa. |

# 2

# *Bacterial Morphology*

Morphology depicts bacterial shape, size, arrangement and structure. Most bacteria are 0.5-1 μ in diameter, their shape can be spherical (cocci), straight rods (bacilli) or straight rods that are helically curved (spirilium); some may exhibit varying shapes and are called pleomorphic. Cocci appear in several characteristic arrangements depending on plane of cell division. Bacilli are not arranged in patterns as complex as cocci and most occur singly or in pairs (diplobacilli); *Bacillus subtilis* forms chains. Staphylococci divide in three planes in an irregular pattern forming bunches of grapes. Strepto cocci divide in one plane and form chains. Diplococci divide in one plane and remain in pairs. Tetracocci divide in *Two* planes and form group of four cells. Bacteria with less than one complete twist or curve have a vibrioid shape while those with one or more complete turns have helical shape. Besides the above common shapes - other shapes seen less frequently are pear shaped *(Pasteuria)*; lobed spheres *(Sulphalobus)*, rods with squared ends *(Bacillus anthracis)*; disks arranged like sacks of coins *(Caryphanon)*; rods with helically sculptured surfaces *(Seliberia)*. Structures external to the bacterial cell wall are pili, flagella and capsule. The flagella are hair like helical appendages imparting motility. They can be polar or lateral. A flagellum has 3 parts - basal body associated with cytoplasmic body; a short hook and a helical filament. The hook and helical filament contain protein flagellin. Unlike hair the flagellum grows at its tip rather than the base. Bacteria propel themselves by rotating their helical flagella

Bacteria having polar flagella move in a back and forth fashion. Bacteria having lateral flagella have a complex movement. Certain helical bacteria like spirochetes exhibit swarming motility even though they lack external flagella but have periplasmic flagella. Bacteria have chemoreceptors located on cytoplasmic memberane which influences bacterial movement towards or away from a substance. Phototropic bacteria move towards increasing light intensities.

*Pili* are hollow nonhelical filamentous appendages which have no function in motility but act for entry of genetic material and for attachment of bacteria to human tissues. *Bacterial Capsule* has following functions (1) prevent drying (2) block attachment of bacteriophage (3) antiphagocytic (4) promote bacterial attachment to certain surfaces (5) promote bacterial stability by preventing aggregation and settling down. Some organisms have sheaths, a hollow tube, which when inpregnated with ferric and manganese salts impart strength to the sheath.

The rigid *Cell Wall* imparts shape to the organism. By preventing uptake of water it prevents bacterial swelling and lysis. The peptidoglycan or muracin of cell wall is an insoluble, porous, cross tinked polymer of high strength and rigidity. It is basically a polymer of N-acetyl glucosamine, N-acetyl muramic acid, L-alanine, and D glutamate. Cell wall of archeobacteria contains instead glycoproteins or polysaccharides. In Gram positive bacteria cell wall peptidoglycan content is very high. *Staphylococcus aureus* and *Streptococcus faecalis* have techoic acid in their cell wall. (peptidoglycan covalently linked to ribitol / glycerol phosphate). Walls of *Streptococcus pyogenes* contains polysaccharides. In gram negative bacteria the cell wall is more complex; a thin outer membrane surrounds the underlying layer of peptidoglycan; the former forming an impermeable barrier for inner enzymes to escape. The outer membrane of the gram negative cell wall is anchored to the underlying peptidoglycan by means of Braun's lipoprotein. The membrane is a bilayered structure consisting mainly of phospholipids, proteins and lipo polysaccharides. The lipopolysaccharide is the endotoxin and consists of lipid. A, poly saccharide and O antigens. Although impermeable to large molecules like proteins; nucleosides, olisosaccharides, aminoacids and peptide can pass through special channels called porins.

Immediately beneath the cell wall lies the cytoplasmic membrane. It is 7.5 nm thick, composed of proteins (60-70%) and phospholipids (20-30%). The phospholipids form a bilayer in which most of the proteins are tenaciously held (integral proteins) and can not be easily removed. Other proteins are only loosely attached. The phospholipids of eubacteria are phosphoglycerides in which straight chain fatty acid are ester linked to glycerol but in archeobacteria, the lipids are poly isoprinoid branched-chain lipids, in which long chain branched alcohols (phytanols) are ether linked to glycerol. The cytoplasmic membrane is a hydrophobic barrier to penetration by most water soluble molecules. This membrane contains various enzymes involved in respiratory metabolism and in synthesis of capsular and cell wall components.

Protoplast is that portion of a bacterial cell consisting of cytoplasmic membrane and the cell material bounded by it. Propoplasts can be prepared from gram positive bacteria by treating the bacteria with lysozyme or culturing bacteria in presence of penicillen that prevents cell wall synthesis. Spcroplast refers to the gram negative bacteria without the outer cell wall but intact cytoplasmic membrane and the outer membrane encircling it. This outer membrane is absent in gram positive bacteria. Mycoplasma do not of have cell wall and are bounded by cytoplasmic membrane.

Bacteria do not contain membrane enclosed organelles corresponding to mitochondria and chloroplasts of eucaryotic cells. They have membrane invaginating in the form of systems of convoluted tubules and vesicles termed *Mesosomes* which are either central or peripheral. The cytoplasm contains RNA protein bodies called ribosomes, DNA, and the cytoplasmic fluid in which are dissolved the macromolecules. There is no endoplasnic reticulum in bacteria. The granules present in cytoplasm are the volutin granules (metachormatic), glycogen granules and poly beta hydroxybutyrate and sulphate.

In contrast to eucaryotic cells, bacteria contain neither a distinct membrane enclosed nucleus, nor a mitotic apparatus. However, they do contain an area near the center of the cell containing DNA which is single and circular containing all the bacterial genes.

Certain bacteria produce spores - either within the cell (*endospore*) or external to the cell (*exospore*). Spores are metabolically dormant but grow to vegetative form under appropriate condition and spores are heat resistant and resist desication. They contain large amounts of dipicolinic acid (DPA) eg. in clostridia. Cells of methane oxidizing genus have exospores but they lack DPA. In actinomycetes spores form singly or in chains from the branching hyphae and are called conidiospores (lack enclosing sac) or sporangiospores (have enclosing sac).

## Spore forming bacteria

- *Bacillus anthracis* and *Bacillus subtilis*
- *Clostridium tetani*, *Clostridium botulinum* and *Clostridium perfringens.*
- *Coxiella burnetti*

## Gram stain

First described by Gram in 1884, it is used to study morphologic appearance of bacteria. Some organisms are not decolorized and retain colour of basic stain like gentian violet, while others lose gentian violet when treated with decolourizing agent like acetone or alcohol. They take up the counter stains like dilute carbol fuchsin or safranin.

Procedure for gram staining is as follows. The bacterial suspension is spread as a thin film on a greaseless clean glass slide and is allowed to dry in the air. Then it is fixed by passing the slide over the flame for 2-3 minutes. Then gentian violet is put on the slide for 1-2 minute followed by Gram's iodine. The smear is then decolorized with acetone or alcohol and washed in water. The smear is then counterstained with 0.5% safranin or 1:20 dilute carbolfuchsin for 1-2 minute. Finally the smear is washed in water, airdried and seen under oil imersion lens. The iodine helps in holding the gentian violet by cell wall of gram positive organism. Routine gramstain requires atleast $10^5$ bacilli/ml (almost close to the limit of visible turbidity in liquid media) to make microscopic detection possible.

## Acidic acridine orange stain

It makes bacterial detection much easier. Bacteria fluoresce under ultraviolet light as red orange forms against greenish leucocytes and unstained erythrocytes.

## Albert stain

Some bacteria like *Corynebacterium diphtheriae* have metachromatic black granules which stain dark bluish or black with methylene blue or a mixture of malachite green and toludine blue. The heat fixed smear be covered with Albert stain I for 5-7 minutes followed by Albert stain II for another 5 minutes. Then the smear is washed under tap water and air dried. The body of bacilli look green while granules take bluish-black colour.

### Ziehl-Neelsen Stain

It is used for acid fast organisms. Some organisms retain carbol fuchsin even when decolorised with acid. The heat fixed smear is stained with carbol fuchsin and the slide is heated and kept for 8-10 minutes. Then the smear is decolourized with 3% HCl in 95% ethyl alcohol or 20% $H_2SO_4$. The slide is then washed under tap water and is counter stained with methylene blue or melachite green. Acid fast organisms that contain mycolic acid in their cell wall resist decolourization, retain carbol fuchsin and appear red. Acid fast organisms include *Mycobacterium tuberculosis* and *Mycobacterium leprae*, bacterial spores, nocardia, actinomyces and exoskeleton of insects.

### Capsular stains

The bacterial capsules do nor stain with ordinary anilinc dyes. In Gram stain the capsule appears as an area of halo around the bacteria. Capsule is rapidly demonstrated in India ink preparation, when it is seen as clear halo between refractile outline of cell wall and greyish background of India ink. The capsule stains blue when the freshly prepared smear is treated with hot crystal violet for one minute and is then washed with 20% copper sulphate.

### Spore stain

Spores are resistant to ordinary method of staining. In Gram stain they appear as clear areas in deeply stained body of the organism. Modified acid fast stains can demonstrate the spores. The heat fixed smear is treated with steaming carbol fuchsin for 3-6 minutes, then decolourized with

0.5% $H_2SO_4$ or 2% nitric acid in absolute alcohol. Then it is washed with water and counter stained with 1% methylene blue. Spores stain bright red and vegetative part of the bacillus blue.

# 3

## *Bacterial Metabolism*

For growth bacteria require oxygen, optimum temperature and pH and adequate nutrients. Bacteria can be (1) phototrophics i.e.; get energy from photochemical reaction or (2) chemotrophics i.e.; get energy from chemical reaction. Based on their ability to synthesize essential metabolites they can be (a) autotrophics i.e.; synthesize all essential metabolites from $CO_2$ and other inorganic salts like nitrites, nitrates, phosphates (b) heterotrophics - i.e.; depend upon supply of growth factors form outside like aminoacid, peptones, proteins and vitamins. Most of the bacteria causing disease in humans are heterotrophic.

The essential elements required for synthesis of bacterial structural component like carbohydrate, fat, protein, nucleic acid include carbon, nitrogen, hydrogen, oxygen, phosphorus and sulfur. Hydrogen and oxygen are made available from water. Ammonia is main source of nitrogen, essential for protein and nucleic acid synthesis. Sulfur is derived from sulphates and it is part of several coenzymes. Phosphorus is assimilated as free inorganic phosphate and is essential for synthesis of nuclcic acids, NADP, ATP etc. Mineral salts required for bacterial growth include potassium, calcium, iron, copper, magnesium, molybdenum and zinc.

The capacity of bacteria to grow in the presence of oxygen and to utilize it depends upon possession of cytochrome oxidase system. *Aerobes* only grow in presence of oxygen. *Facultative anaerobes* are those that can live with or without oxygen eg ;- vibrio, salmonella, shigella, escherichia and staphylococci. *Obligate anaerobes* only grow in absence of oxygen. e.g. Clostridia, bacteroides. Micro aerophilic organisms grow well in presence of small quantity of oxygen. e.g.; haemophilus. Aerobes contain superoxide dismutase and catalase that neutralise the free radicals like hydrogen peroxide and superoxide liberated from reduction of oxygen by flavoproteins. Lactic acid bacteria and aerotolerant anaerobes do not contain superoxide dismutase and catalase but instead peroxidase. All strict anaerobes do not contain free radical neutralising enzymes.

Hydrogen peroxides damages DNA. *Rec A* gene product repairs DNA and is more important than catalase and superoxide dismutase in protecting *E.coli.* against $H_2O_2$ toxicity. *N. gonorrhoae* and *B. abortus* grow well in presence of extra $CO_2$ in culture medium.

**Accessory nutritional requirement**

| | | |
|---|---|---|
| *N. gonorrhoea* | – | Glutathione |
| *C. diphtheriae* | – | B-alanine |
| *S. aureus* | – | Thiamine, nicotinic acid |
| *H. influenzae* | – | Haematin |

These growth promoting agents are not synthesized by bacteria, hence be supplied from outside. Bacterial growth in body besides nutritional needs depends upon pH, redox potential, cellular and humoral defence and generation time of bacteria.

Bacterical growth curve has lag phase, log phase, stationary phase, decline phase and survival phase. The *Lag Phase* has duration of 1-40 hours in which there is increase in size of the cell as well as mctabolic activity. The *Log phase* has duration of 8 hours and the bacterial division proceeds in geometric fashion. *Stationary phase* lasts from few hours to few days. Bacterial multiplication in balanced by equal destruction due to nutritional depletion and accumulation of toxic products. There after the *Decline phase* starts to end in survival phase where a few bacteria are left with. The optimum temperature for bacterial growth is 30°C - 37°C. Soil and water bacteria grow at 0°C - 25°C and are called *psychrophilic*; those growing between 50°C - 60°C are called *thermophilic* e.g. algae and those growing between 20°C - 44°C — *mesophilic* that produce most human disease. Optimum pH for bacterial growth is 7.2-7.6. However vibrios grow in alkaline pH and lactobacilli in acidic pH. *N gonorrhoeae* and *T. pallidum* die without moisture while *S. aureus* and mycobacteria survive long in absence of moisture. Most bacteria are resistant to changes in osmotic pressure but 0.5% NaCl is added to most culture media to make the environment isotonic. Darkness favors bacterial growth and viability. Photochromogenic mycobacteria produce pigment in light. UV and other forms of radiation kill most bacteria. Though bacteria have tough cell walls vigorous shaking or ultrasonic vibration can disrupt the cell wall. Time requried for bacterium to divide to two daughter cells is the *generation time*. For coliforms it is 20 minutes, for *M tuberculosis* - 20 minutes and *M leprae* - 20 days.

Bacteria are metabolically more active due to relatively large surface area through which nutrients are readily absorbed. The substrates utilized and the end products vary in different groups of organisms. Aerobes obtain energy by oxidative phosphorylation with $CO_2$ and $H_2O$ being end products and generation of ATP. Anaerobes obtain energy by fermentation with production of alcohol, acid and gas (hydrogen and $CO_2$) as end products. Facultative anaerobes may obtain their energy exclusively by fermentation (streptococci) or respiration (entero bacteria). However the amount of ATP generated under anaerobic conditions is less. Redox potential *(Eh)* i.e. capability to accept or donate electrons, of most media in contact with air is +2 to +0.4 mv. at pH 7. Degradation of glucose varies in different bacteria. The end products of glucose fermentation are $CO_2$, $H_2$, acetic, formic, lactic and pyruvic acids and alcohol. Production of acid with or without gas is used in identification of bacteria. Polysaccharides in the environment are broken down by exoenzymes to liberate glucose which then enters the bacteria to be acted upon by endoenzymes for liberation of energy. Proteases similarly breakdown peptides into amino acids which enters cell for protein synthesis.

Bacterial metabolism in linked to presence and synthesis of key enzymes of respiratory chain and other metabolic events. Enzyme is mostly protein with other chemical groups. An apoenzyme when combined with a coenzyme forms an complete enzyme or holoenzyme Many coenzymes are vitamin derivatives.

| *Vitamin* | *Coenzyme* |
|---|---|
| Thiamine ($B_1$) | Cocarboxylase |
| Riboflavin ($B_2$) | Riboflavin adenine dinucleotide |
| Niacin | Nicotinamide adenine dinucleotide |
| Pyridoxine ($B_6$) | Pyridoxal phosphate |
| Folic acid | Tetrahydrofolic acid |

The non protein portion of an enzyme can be metal like $Mg^{++}$, $Mn^{++}$, $Fe^{++}$, $Zn^{++}$. These metal ions are cofactors. Some enzymes require comfactor as well as coenzyme. Catalases use ions as a cofactor. Enzymes can be classified as.

| *Class* | *Catalytic reaction* |
|---|---|
| 1. Oxidoreductases | Electron transfer reactions |
| 2. Transferases | Transfer of functional groups |
| 3. Hydrolases | Hydrolysis (Addition of water molecule) |
| 4. Lyases | Addition to double bonds |

| | |
|---|---|
| 5. Isomerases | Isomeraization reactions |
| 6. Ligases | Formation of bonds with cleavage of ATP |

Enzymes may be divided into two groups-constitutive and inducible. The former is produced always in a cell but later in produced only in response to a particular substrate. Lactose induces synthesis of beta galactosidase. In many bacteria the structural genes governing the biosynthesis of proteins are positioned in the exact order of the sequence of reactions in the particular metabolic pathway. For every structural gene there is operator (Inducer) and repressor segments which control mRNA synthesis by the structural genes. An enzyme inducer is a substrate that needs the enzyme to be synthesized. An enzyme repressor is the substance that acting on operator gene segment inhibits protein synthesis. End product repression is another way of inhibiting enzyme synthesis. When end product of bacterial synthetic pathway is added to culture medium the concerned enzyme synthesis in inhibited. In medium containing both glucose and lactose, glucose in preferentially metabolized by E.coli. The enzymes for catabolism of lactose are not synthesized till all glucose is metabolized. This type of inhibition in called catabolite repression.

**Bioenergetics :** In the course of any chemical reaction energy available for the performance of useful work is either released or absorbed. This is $\Delta G$ or free energy change. When $\Delta G$ is negative the reaction releases energy (exergonic) and when positive the reaction requires energy (endergonic).

$\Delta G^o$ is the amount of free energy released or absorbed when one mole of reactant in converted to one mole of product at 25°C under 1 atmospheric pressure.

$$\Delta G = -RT \text{ in } Keq.$$

Where R is the gas constant, and T is the absolute temperature and Keq. is the equilibrium constant.

Table below lists some of the high energy transfer compounds found in cell, of which, ATP is for the most important and is the "energy currency" of the cell. All the compounds mentioned in the table can transfer their energy directly or indirectly to ATP synthesis e.g., 1,3 diphosphoglyceric acid +ADP = 3 phosphoglyceric acid + ATP

| *Compound* | *$\Delta G^o$ Kcal $mol^{-1}$* |
|---|---|
| Adenosine triphosphate | —7.3 |
| Guanosine triphosphate | —7.3 |
| Uridine triphosphate | —7.3 |
| Cytidine triphosphate | —7.3 |
| Acetyl phosphate | —10.1 |
| 1-3 Diphosphoglyceric acid | —11.8 |
| Phosphophenol pyruvic acid | —14.8 |

*Hydrolysis of Adenosine Compounds*

ATP + $H_2O \rightarrow$ ADP + $H_2PO_4$, $\Delta G^o$ = —7.3 Kcal $mol^{-1}$

ADP + $H_2O \rightarrow$ AMP + $H_3PO_4$, $\Delta G^o$ = -7.3 Kcal $mol^{-1}$

AMP + $H_2O \rightarrow$ Adenosine + $H_3PO_4$, $\Delta G^o$ = —2 Kcal

**Oxidation - Reduction reactions**

Oxidation is the loss of electron, reduction is the gain of electrons Frequently oxidation reactions are dehydrogenation in nature, since hydrogen atom consists of one proton and one electron. An oxidizing agent will absorb the lost electron. and will therefore will be reduced. The ferric ion is an oxidizing agents as it absorbs electron and becomes reduced to ferrous ion. A reducing agent donates electrons, becoming oxidized in the process. Electron transport chains are sequences of oxidation reduction reactions. As the electrons flow through the chain their free energy in conserved in the form of ATP — a process called oxidative phosphorylation. The multicomponent electron transport chains are always associated with membranes—mitochondrial membranes in eucaryocytes and cytoplasmic membrane in procaryocytes. A respiratory chain consists of enzymes having prosthetic groups or coenzyme. The coenzymes involved are NAD, FAD, Coenzyme Q, and cytochromes. Cytochrome is a heme derivative with single iron atom. The cytochromes act sequentially to transport electrons from coenzymes Q to $O_2$. The arrangement of oxidation reduction systems is according to Eo' values starting from $NAD^+/NADH$ which in —0.32, increasing gradually to Cyt b, Cyt.C1, CytC, Cyta and finally $Cyta_3$ (whose Eo' value is +0.53.

Micro organism mostly catabolize glucose by Embden Meherhof pathway. It does not require oxygen and can occur in both aerobic and anaerobic bacteria.

$C_6H_2O_6$ + 2 NAD + 2ADP + 2P. → $2CH_3COCOOH$ + $2NADH_2$ + 2ATP

Glucose Inorganic phosphate (Pyruvic acid)

**In pentose phosphate pathway**

Glucose - 6 - phosphate + 12 NADP→ $6CO_2$ + 12 NADPH + $12H^+$ + Pi

However it is not major pathway of energy production in bacteria. It rather provides NADPH and $H^+$ which are required in other biosynthetic reactions.

Another pathway of glucose catabolism is Enter - Dou - doroff pathway which is common in Gram negative bacteria producing pyruvic acid and acetyl CoA.

Pyruvic acid is regarded as the key compound in the dissimilation of glucose. Tricarboxylic acid cycle is the sequence of reactions that generate energy in the form of ATP and reduced $NADH_2$ and $FADH_2$. Many intermediates in the cycle are precursor in the biosynthesis of aminoacids, pyrimidines etc. Thus TCA cycle is amphibolic (both catabolic and anabolic). The overall reaction of TCA cycle is

$$\text{Acetyl COA} + 3H_2O + 3\ NAD^+ + FAD + ADP + P_1 \rightarrow$$
$$2CO_2 + COA + 3\ NADH_2 + FADH_2 + ATP$$

Since breakdown of glucose by glycolysis yields two acetyl COA molecules which enters TCA cycle, the overall equation is twice the above.

i.e. generation of :

| | | | |
|---|---|---|---|
| 6 $NADH_2$ | = | 18 ATP | |
| 2 $FADH_2$ | = | 4 ATP | Total 24 ATP in TCA cycle. |
| 2 GTP | = | 2 ATP | |

Conversion of 2 pyruvic acid to 2 acetyl COA yields 2 NADP (6 ATP); and in EM pathway there is formation of 2 $NADH_2$ (6 ATP) and 2 ATP. So total ATP yield in glucose metabolism is 24 + 6 + 6 + 2 = 38 ATP. Outof 38 ATP, 34 ATP are generated from the reduced coenzymes via oxidative phosphorylation through the respiratory chain.

$$C_6H_2O_6 + 6O_2 = 6\ CO_2 + 6H_2O$$

The glycoxylate cycle is used by some microorganisms when acetate is the sole carbon source or during oxidation of primary substrates (such as higher fatty acids) that are cleaved to acetyl COA without the intermediate formation of pyruvic acid. The specific enzymes of this cycle are isocitrrate lyase and malate synthase.

# 4

# *Growth Media*

Culture media give artificial environment simulating natural conditions necessary for bacterial growth. A culture medium should provide carbon, nitrogen, trace elements, minerals like sodium, potassium, magnesium, iron, calcium and copper with pH of 7.2-7.6 and right redox potential and essential growth factors for specific organisms.

## Fluid media

Bacteria grow well in fluid media in 3-4 hours. Fluid media are not suitable for isolation of organism and study of their colony characteristic. *Broth* is a clear transparent straw coloured fluid prepared from meat extract or peptone. Peptone is partially digested protein and in 1% peptone bacteria grow very well. Yeast extract is another liquid medium. Other liquid media used are - 1% sugar in peptone water, 1% glucose in nutrient broth, bile broth (0.5% bile salts in nutrient broth), Hiss serum (1 part serum and 3 parts glucose broth) liquid Mac Conkey, glycerol saline and enrichment media (tetrathionate and selenite).

## Solid Media

Solid media are used for study of colony characteristic. Agar, a complex polysaccharide derived from sea weeds is most often used. It does not provide any nutrition, nor is metabolized by any pathogenic bacteria; it only acts as a solidfying agent. Gelatin, a protein prepared by hydrolysis of collagen, is liquid at 37°C but forms transparent gel below 25°C. Some bacteria liquefy gelatin and this property helps in their identification. Blackening of gelatin indicates

$H_2S$ production. A simple media consists of meat extract, peptone, sodium chloride and water. Enriched media have added blood, egg; e.g., blood agar, chocolate agar, Loeffler serum slope. Enrichment of media with certain growth factors hastens growth of specific organisms e.g. selenite F broth, tetrathionate broth. Selective media contain inhibiting substances. Some media contain an indicator which changes colour with growth of organisms. Mac Conkey's medium (peptone, lactose, agar, neutral red and taurocholate) shows lactose fermenters as red colonies and non lactose fermenters as pale colonies. Stuart medium for gonococci and glycerol saline for stool are two examples of transport media. Robertson's cooked meat medium is for culture of anaerobic organisms and contains indicator like reduced methylene blue. Bacterial preservation is done in storage media. e.g. dorset egg and semisolid agar.

**Culture methods**

**Streak culture** (Surface plating) is the method routinely employed for bacterial isolation in pure culture. A plantinum loop is charged with specimen to be cultured and is placed towards periphery of a solid media, then spread thinly over the plate in series of parallel lines. Confluent growth occurs at the site of primary inoculum but well separated discrete colonies grow along the parallel lines.

**Carpet culture** is flooding the solid plate with bacterial suspension. It is useful for bacteriophage typing and antibiotic sensitivity testing.

### Stroke culture

Stroke culture is made in tubes containing agar slopes, mainly used for providing bacterial growth for slide agglutination.

### Stab culture

Stab culture is prepared by puncturing with charged long straight wire, mainly employed for demonstrating gelatin liquefaction and for maintaining stock culture.

### Pure plate culture

It is used to provide viable bacterial count in a suspension and is the recommended method for quantitative urine culture. 15 ml of agar medium is melted and left to cool in water both at 45-50°C. Appropriate dilution of the inoculum is added in 1 ml volume to molten agar and mixed well. Content of the tube is poured into petridish and is allowed to set. After incubation colonies will be seen distributed through out the depth of the medium.

### Liquid culture

Liquid culture in a tube, bottle or flask may be inoculated by touching with a charged loop. It is prefered when large and quick yield is required. However it does not provide pure culture from mixed inocula.

### Colony characteristics

The *shape* may be circular, irregular, radiate or rhizoid.

The *surface* may be smooth, rough, fine or coarsely granular, papillate, glistening

The *size* may vary from 0.5 mm to 3 mm

The *elevation* may be raised, low convex, dome, umbilicated

The *edges* may be entire (e.g. Klebsiella, *E. coli*, *Staph aureus)*, undulate, lobate, erose, crenated, effuse and fimbriated *(B. subtilis)*

The *colour* is due to production of pigments as in pseudomonas and staphylococci.

The *opacity* of colonies on nutrient agar may be transparent, translueent or opaque

The *consistency* of colonies may be hard or firm (e.g., *Mycobacterium tuberculosis)*; friable and membranous (e.g.; *B subtilis*); soft and butyrous (e.g., *E. coli*)

Some bacteria produce spreading growth e.g., proteus and clostridia._*Staphylococcus Aureus* and *Streptococcus pyogenes* cause beta haemolysis around the colony.

**Emulsifiability**

Growth of *E. coli*, salmonella, is easily emulsifiable where as growth of *Neisseria catarrhalis* is not.

Growth in *liquid media* can be described as turbid, deposit at the bottom (*S. pyogenes*), surface growth (mainly in aerobes), colour changes (pseuedomonas) due to water soluble pigment production.

**Anaerobic culture**

Obligate anaerobes only grow in absence of oxygen. They lack machanism of oxidation through respiratory enzymes like cytochrome oxidase, catalase and peroxidase *Anaerobiosis* can be achieved by exclusion of oxygen, - production of vacuum, displacement of oxygen with other gases, absorption of oxygen by chemical / biological means or reduction of oxygen. Vacuum is never complete so also displacement of $O_2$ wih $CO_2$, $N_2$, and helium. Absorption of oxygen by sodium hydroxide, pyrogellic acid can be tried but GASPAK is now the standard method consisting of an envelop placed in a jar. The envelop contains one tablet each of citric acid, sodium carbonate and sodium borohydrate. It generates $H_2$, $CO_2$; the hydrogen combining with oxygen to form water.

*Macinstosh and Fildes* anaerobic jar is an alternative which is an airtight metal jar with outlet and inlet, the outlet tube is connected to vaccum pumps and air inside is evalcuated. Through inlet tube hydrogen is filled inside this jar. The palladinised asbestos inside jar is then electrically heated which consumes hydrogen and residual oxygen if any within the jar. It ensures complete anaerobiosis but carries the risk of explosion. Methylene blue is used as indicator, which remains colourless in anaerobiosis but turns blue if there is residual $O_2$ within the jar. *Anaerobic glove box* is an expensive self contained anaerobic system with provisions of circulation of $H_2$, $N_2$ and $CO_2$ within it and catalytic conversion of residual $O_2$ to water.

Reduction of oxygen in the medium can be achieved by using 1% glucose, 0.1% ascorbic acid / thioglycolate, 0.05% cystine.

# 5

## *Bacterial Classification and Identification*

A number of criteria have been employed to classify the bacteria

1. Energy source - Phototrophic, chemotrophic, autotrophic, heterotrophic
2. Oxygen requirement - Aerobic, anaerobic
3. Temperature for growth - Thermophilic, mesophilic and psychrophilic
4. Nutrient requirement - Simple and complex
5. Ability to grow in living tissue - Saprophytes and parasites

True bacteria are unicellular and never form mycelium.

(1) Based on their shape they can be cocci, (spherical), bacilli (rod shaped), vibrio (comma shaped), spirilla (spiral twisted nonflexous rods) and spirochaetes (thin spirally twisted flexous rods). Cocci, based on their arrangement can be diplococci (e.g.; pneumococci), occurring in chains (streptococci), arranged in cluster (staphylococci) and arranged in group of 4 (*Micrococcus teragena*)

(2) Based on Gram stain cocci can be gram positive or Gram negative

*Gram positive cocci* - Staphylococcus, Streptococcus, pnuemo coccus, micrococcus, sarcinecoccus

*Gram negative cocci* - Grnococcus, meningococcus.

Bacilli similarly can be gram positive or gram negative; motile or non motile, anaerobic and aerobic, spore bearing and nonspore bearing

*Gram negative bacilli* - Enterobacteria,

pseudomonads, Brucella, Bacteroides, Haemophilus, Klebsiella, pasteurella, proteus.

*Gram Positive Bacilli* - Corynebacteria, mycobacteria, lactobacillus, clostridia,

*Gram Negative Motile Bacilli* - Vibrio, salmonella, *E-coli,* proteus, pseudomonas, citrobacter,

Gram positive motile bacilli - Clostridia, *B. anthracis*

Gram positive spore forming bacilli —

(a) Aerobic - *B. anthracis, B. subtilis*

(b) Anaerobic - Clostridia

The spirochaetes are slender, refractile and spiral filaments. They have three genera - treponema, leptospira and borrelia.

(3) *Adansonian classification* - This system determines the degrees of relationship between strains by a statistical coefficient. The different organisms are compared by comparing for a number of phenotypic characteristics.

(4) *Biochemical classification* - It hinges on the chemical composition of cell wall. N-acetyl muramic acid does not occur in eukaryotic cell and sterols are lacking in prokaryotic cell. Gram positive bacteria contain glycerol and ribitol, techoic acid along with mannose and rhamanose.

(5) *DNA composition* - The guanine + cytosine composition is relatively fixed or fall within a very narrow range for one species of bacteria and thus provides a means of classifying them.

## Bacterial Identification

Bacterial identification is based on microscopic examination for shape, size, motility, spores and study of staining properties, cultural characteristics and biochemical reaction.

The biochemical reactions are the widely used tests.

1. *Sugar Fermentation* by some bacteria yields acid changing the Andrade's indicator red. The gas produced collects in Durham's tube
2. *Indole Production* - Indole is produced from tryptophan present in the peptone water. When Kovac reagent is added a red colour ring develops.
3. *Methyl Red Test* - It indicates fermentation of glucose. 0.04% methyl red when added to the medium red colour develops signalling presence of acid
4. *Voges - Proskauer Test* - It depends upon production of acetyl methyl carbinol from pyruvic acid. To 48 hours growth of glucose phosphate culture 40% KOH (1 volume) with 3 volumes of naphthal are added. A deep pink colour turning to magenta or cirmson red indicate positive test.
5. *Citrate Utilization* - Koser citrate medium is used for this test. Turbidity if develops indicates utilization of citrate. In Simon's (solid) medium change of colour from green to blue indicates citrate utilization.
6. *Nitrate Reduction* - Broth containing 1% $KNO_3$ is incubated for 5 days. To it are added mixture of 1-2 drops of sulfanilic acid and naphthalamine when red colour appears in few minutes.
7. *Urease Test* - Urease producing organisms reduce urea to ammonia and produce pink colour in Christensen's usease medium
8. *Hydrogen Sulfide Production* is from decomposition of sulfur containing amino acids. It turns lead acetate paper strips into black.
9. *Catalase Production* - A glass slide with 10 drops of

$H_2O_2$ is charged with bacterial colony. In a positive test gas bubbles evolve.

10. *Oxidase Reactions* - The bacterial colony is smeared over paper soaked with tetramethyl-p-phenylene diamine hydrochloride. In positive case the smear turns dark purple in 5-10 seconds.
11. Growth in KCN - 1 in 13000 dilution of KCN is needed to identify gram negative bacilli
12. *Hippurate Hydrolysis* test is based on hydrolysis of benzyl glycine (hippurate) to benzene and glycine, detected by addition of ferric chloride, positive in *Klebsiella*
13. *ONPG* (O-nitrophenyl-beta-galactopyranoside) *test* is used to detect enzyme betagalactosidase present in lactose fermenters like *E. coli*. ONPG is broken down to release O-nitrophenol giving yellow colour.
14. *Antigenic Analysis* is based on use of specific antisera in agglutination reaction. Betahaemolytic streptococcus can be differentiated into 18 serological groups based on polysaccharide antigen; and pheumococci into 77 types based on its capsular properties with specific antisera.

*Bacteriophages Typing*

Bacteriophages are viruses that parasitize bacteria bringing about their lysis. Phage typing is useful in distinguising strains of salmonella and staphylococci.

*Newer Methods*

Bacterial detection in pathological samples can be made by (i) gas liquid chromatography (ii) Counter current immunoelectrophoresis (iii) luminescent biometry (iv) radio respirometry (v) genetic probes (vi) eletrical impedance measurement of sample etc.

# 6

# *Sterilization and Disinfection*

*Sterilization* is the process by which articles are freed of all microorganisms, both vegetative and spore forms. *Disinfection* is the process of destruction of pathogenic organisms.

*Antiseptices* prevent growth of microorganism. Bacterio-static agents only prevent multiplication of bacteria while bacteriocidal agents kill the microbes.

| *Physical* | *Chemicals* |
|---|---|
| Sunlight | Acids, alkalies |
| Heat | Halogens |
| moist & dry | |
| Filtration | Oxidising and reducing agents |
| Radiation | Formal dehyde |
| Ultrasonic vibrations | Phenol, soaps, dyes |

Ultraviolet rays in sunlight cause natural disinfection. Drying kills many bacteria but not their spores. Dry heat causes protein denaturation and oxidative damage. Red heat is used to sterilize metallic objects by holding them in flame till red hot. In flaming the article to be sterilized is only passed over the flame. Incineration destroys hospital waste but production of dioxin may cause cancer and sterility. Hot airoven requires temperature of 160°C for an hour and can sterilize glass syringes, flasks, pipettes, cotton swabs, liquid paraffin, dusting powder, test tubes, scissors, scalpels etc. Moist heat can be used in various temperature ranges for disinfection. In *Pasturization* of milk temperature of 63-72°C is maintained for upto 30 minutes followed by sudden cooling. It kills mycobacteria, salmonella and brucella but not coxiella. In sterilization of vaccine the vaccine is treated with moist heat at 60°C for an hour. *Tyndallization* is the process in which the medium is placed at 100°C in flowing steam for 30 minutes daily on 3 successive days. It may be used for sterilization of egg or serum containing media. Boiling kills most vegetative forms of bacteria, fungi and viruses. Addition of little acid, alkali or washing soda increase the sterilizing power of boiling water but spores and HBV are not easily killed. Steam at 100°C and atmospheric pressure is a cheap method of sterilization of culture media. High pressure steam sterilizers and autoclaves are used for sterilization of hospital equipment and linen. In autoclaving steam at 15 lb pressure and at 121°C for 15-20 minutes sterilizes the articles like culture media, rubber goods, syringes, gowns and dressings. Low pressure low temperature autoclaves and high pressure high vacuum autoclaves are available.

Sterilization by filtration is useful for antibiotics, sera but viruses and mycoplasma may pass through the filter. Ultraviolet radiation can kill most organisms but spores are resistant. UV light causen DNA damage, protein denaturation, and formation of $H_2O_2$.

Ionizing radiation is more lethal than UV rays, hence useful for sterilization of catgut, disposable syringes, adhesive dressiangs. A dose of 2 milirad is enough to kill bacteria and their spores. Ozone can sterilize water and vegetables.

Chemical methods of sterilization bring about oxidation and coagulation of bacterial protoplasm, cell membrane disruption, enzyme inactivation etc. Mycobacteria are more resistant to acid than alkalies. *Metallic Ions* like $HgCl_2$ and $AgNO_3$ are effective in concentration less than 1 part per million due to high affinity for proteins Fluoride inhibits many bacterial enzymes. Potassium tellurite is inhibitory to Gram negative bacteria. *Halogens* like. Chlorine, iodine and bromine kill vegetative bacteria, fungi and viruses but not bacterial spores and mycobacteria. Chlorine combines with water to form hypochloric acid which is bactericidal. Potassium permanganate is a weak oxidizing agent. 5-10% *Formal dehyde* kills many bacteria, spores and viruses. It is used to disinfect woolen blankets, wards and operation theatre. 50 ml of 40% formalin can fumigate 100 cft of space when heated with water. Alternately 50% formalin can be sprayed which liberates formal dehyde gas. 3% *Phenol* is bactericidal. It is used to sterilize surgical instruments. *Detergents* also disrupt cell membrane. 70% *ethyl alcohol* is bactericidal but does not kill the spores. Gentian violet and malachite green are active against Gram positive bacteria. 1 in 1000 *acriflavin* is a commonly used bacteriostatic agent. *Propylene glycol* is a strong gaseous disinfectant so also sulphur dioxide.

# 7

# *Bacterial Genetics and Immunity*

## Bacterial Genetics

Genetics is the study of heredity and variation. Human life is coded by the 3 billion letters in our DNA spread over 31,000 gene interacting in an intricate way. Each bacterium contains about 1000 genes located on its circular chromosome. It is only in 1966 that John Cairns explained the duplication of bacterial chromosome but in 1973 Dr HG Khurana produced the first synthetic functional DNA. DNA acts as the template for the synthesis of messenger RNA. Adenine, guanine, cytosine and uracil of RNA are complementary respectively to thymine, cytosine, guanine and adenine in the DNA. Sequence of three bases codes for an amino acid but more than one codon exists for same amino acid. UAA, UAG and UGA donot code for any amino acid and are called nonsense codons. The sequence of nuleotides in a gene determine the sequence of aminoacids to be incorporated for protein synthesis. An RNA polymerase forms a single polyribonucleotide strand called messenger RNA (mRNA) using DNA as a template by the process called transcription. The RNA has a nucleotide seqeuence complementary to one of the strands in DNA double helix of the gene. Aminoacids are enzymatically activated and are transferred to specific adapter molecules of RNA called transfer RNA (tRNA). mRNA and tRNA come together on the surface of ribosome and the amino acids are bond together by peptide linkage until the entire mRNA molecule is translated, the process being called translation.

The proteins thus formed are further modified by proof reading.

## Plasmids

It is free circular DNA in bacterial cytoplasm reproducing independently. Plasmids may be conjugative or nonconjugative. Some plasmids can integrate with host chromosomes and some are self transferable. Two members of same group of plasmids cannot coexist in the same cell. Plasmids are lost spontaneously or by curing agents. *Episomes* are genetic elements existing autonomoulsy in the cytoplasm or intergrated in bacterial chromosomes. Plasmids and episomes are not essential for bacterial life but confer properties like toxigenicity, virulence, drug resistance and fertility factor. Plasmid determines penicllinase production by *Staph aureus.* Plasmids are known to encode enzymes of special catabolic pathways (pseudomonas) and enzymes of nitrogen fixation (klebsiella). Fertility factor (F), colicinogenic factor (C) and resistance factor (RTF) are spontaneously transferable. Plasmids based on molecular size can be small (1-10 megadalton) or large (25-300 megadalton). Small plasmids are nonconjugative, non transferable with multiple copies and encode for small number of proteins. Large plasmids are usually conjugative with few copies, self transferable and encode for larger number of proteins.

Like human cells bacteria can have phenotypic and genotypic variation. Phenotypic variations are temporary and readily reversible e.g., change in environmental conditions. Two important phenotypic variations are change in morphology (Spore and capsule formation) and modification in physiological and biochemical characteristics. Virulence is associated with smooth type of colony except tubercle bacilli. Pigment production by certain bacteria is often temperature specific Genotypic variation is due to mutation in nucleotide sequence that passes from one generation to the other. Mutation can be a (i) point mutation where a single base pair has been substituted for another or (ii) multisite mutation. Point mutation can be transition type and frame shift mutation while multisite mutation can be deletion, addition, duplication, inversion etc. Mutation can occur spontaneousely or by mutagenic agents. Spontaneous mutation occurs at a constant rate. i.e. one mu-tation per $10^7$-$10^{10}$ divisions per cell. This leads to attenuation of virulence, loss of sensitivity to bacteriophages, drug resistance, loss of capability to form capsule (pneumococcus) and flagella (salmonella, proteus). Induced mutation by mutagenic agents include physical agents (radilation) or chemical compounds (polycyclic aromatic hydrocarbons, alkylating agents, nitroso compounds, anticancer drugs).

As a result of mutation, there may be alteration in colonial morphology or pigmentation, variation in cell surface antigens, change in virulence and capability to utilize nutrients. Mutation can be proved by (1) fluctuaction test (2) replica testing method and (3) spreading experiments.

Transmission of genetic material in bacteria occurs by (1) transfromation (2) transduction (3) lysogenic conversion (4) conjugation etc. Transformation refers to transfer of genetic material through free DNA, amply demonstrated in pneumococci, haemophilus and neisseria. In transduction bacteriophage transfer a portion of DNA from one bacterium to another. In lysogenic conversion the phage confers new properties to its infected host. In conjugation the male or donor bacterium transfers genetic material to the female or recipient bacterium. The capacity of a strain to act as a donor is determined by fertility factor (F) in cytoplasm. Protoplasmic fusion may occur in osmotically buffered environment. Fusion may occur among members of various unrelated or related cells; the gene tranfer by this method is often called genetic transfusion.

**Probe**

It is a labelled single stranded DNA fragment (20-25 nuclcotide long) which will hybridize with and thereby will detect and locate complementary sequences among the DNA fragment on a Southeren blot. Southeren blot is a technique of transfering DNA fragments which have been separated by electrophoresis on an agar gel, to a nitrocellulose filter, where they can hybridize with probe. Diagnostic DNA probes are available for many (i) bacteria (legionella, mycoplasma, *H. pylori*, *M. tuberculosis*, *E.coli*, MAC) (ii) viruses (HBV, HSV, HIV) and (iii) protozoa (*P. falciparum)*. Betaglobin probe for sickel cell disease and beta thalassemia, alfa globin probe for alpha thalassemia, factor VIII probe for haemophilia, dystrophin probe for Duchenne dystrophy CFTR probe for cystic fibrosis, CAG repeat (Huntigrin) probe for Huntington's disease are available.

**Polymerase chain reaction (PCR)**

It is an invitro method of amplifying the small fragments of DNA present in a specimen. It involves melting of DNA to single stranded DNA, annealing of primers to target DNA and synthesis of DNA by addition of nuclceotide from primers by action of polymerase. PCR diagnosis is quick and can be applied for diagnosis of CNS infection, HBV, HCV, leptospirosis, lyme disease, pneumocystosis, toxoplasmosis, viral infections including HIV and whipple disease.

## Blotting technique (Southern blotting)

DNA fragments obtained by restriction enzyme digestion and separation on gel can be transfered from the gel by blotting to nitrocellulose or nylon membranes that bind the DNA. The DNA bound to the membrae is denatured i.e., converted to single stranded form and treated with radio active single stranded DNA probes. These will hybridize with homologous DNA to form radioactive double stranded segments which can be detected on X-ray films.

## Immune blotting

The protein antigen mixture is separated by sodium dodecyle sulphate polyacrylamide gel electrophoresis blotted into nitrocellulose strips and identified by radiolabelled antibodies on probes. *Dot hybridization* is highly sensitive and specific. DNA of microbe in specimen is spotted on nitrocellulose membrane, where it is bounded and denatured with alkali. The dot is hybridized with radioactive labelled DNA fragment from which DNA probes are prepared. The dot is then autoradiographed.

## Antign-antibody reactions

Antigun-antibody reactions are useful in laboratory diagnosis of various diseases and in identification of infectious agents. These reactions are - agglutination, precipitation and complement fixation. Features of such reactions include (1) entire antigen molecule takes part in the reaction - not fragments (2) there is no denaturation of antigen or antibody (3) combinations occur at the surface (4) the combination is firm but reversible.

**Table 8.1 : Comparative efficiency of immunoglobulins in serological reactions**

| *Reactions* | *Ig G* | *Ig M* | *Ig A* |
|---|---|---|---|
| Preiepitation | Strong | Weak | Variable |
| Agglutination | Weak | Strong | Moderate |
| Complement fixation | Weak | Strong | Negtive |
| Lysis | Weak | Strong | Negative |

## Agglutination

When a particulate antigen is mixed with corresponding antibody in presence of electrolytes at a suitable pH and temperature, agglutination or clumping occurs. It is more sensitive than precipitation. Micro agglutination is carried by mixing a drop of antigen and antiserum. Reaction occurs immediately. It is employed for blood grouping, Rh typing and detection of bacterial antigens. Macroagglutination is carried out as quantitative test for titre of antibody against flagellar antigen, somatic antigen and *vi* antigens.

# 8

# *Systemic Bacteriology*

## SYNONYMS

| | | |
|---|---|---|
| Bang's bacillus | — | Brucella abortus |
| Battey's bacillus | — | Mycobacterium nitrocell-ulosae |
| Bordet Gengou bacillus | — | Bordetella pertusis |
| Butter bacillus | — | Clostridium butyricum |
| Ducrey's bacillus | — | Hemophilus ducreyi |
| Flexner's bacillus | — | Shigella flexneri |
| Friedlander's bacillus | — | Klebsiella pneumoniae |
| Frisch bacillus | — | Klebsiella rhinosclero-matis |
| Gartner's bacillus | — | Salmonella enteritidis |
| Ghon - Sach's bacillus | — | Clostridium septicum |
| Hofman's bacillus | — | Corynebacterium psuedodiphtheriticum |
| Johne's bacillus | — | Mycobacterium paratuber culosis |
| Koch - Week's bacillus | — | Haemophilus aegypticus |
| Pfeiffer's bacillus | — | Haemophilus influenzae |
| Preisz Nocard bacillus | — | Corynebactrium psuedo tuberculosis |
| Schmitz's bacillus | — | Fusobaterium necrophorum |
| Schmitz's bacillus | — | Shigella dysenteriae type - II |
| Strong's bacillus | — | Shigella flexnerae |
| Week's bacillus | — | Haemophilus aegypticus |
| Welch's bacillus | — | Clostridium prefringens |

## *STAPHYLOCOCCUS*

The family micrococcoceae has 3 genera - namely - micrococci, planococci and staptylococci - Micrococci are present on skin and mucous membrane and donot produce disease. Planococci are motile arranged in tetrads. They produce yellow brown pigment on nutrient agar but donot cause any disease. The staphylococcus genus has 30 species of which 14 species are associated with man and animals. Staphylococci were first seen in pus in 1878 by Robert Koch; were cultured by Pasteur in 1880 and were named by A. Ogston in 1881.

### General characteristics

Staphylococci are gram positive nonmotile, ovoid or spheroidal, arranged in groups. On nutrient agar they produce colonies - white, yellow or golden yellow in colour. Pathogenic strains produce coagulase, ferment sugar (glucose, lactose, mannitol) with production of acid, liquefy gelatin and produce pus in lesions. When exposed to chemicals like penicillin they change to L-form. They are not affected by bile salts or optochin.

### Classification

(i) On the basis of pigment production – *Staphy lococcus aureus* produces golden yellow colonies; *Staphylococcus albus* produces white colonies and *Staphylococcus citreus* produces lemon-yellow colonies (ii) On the basis of pathogenicity - pathogenic species like *Steph aureus* and non pathogenic species like *Staph epidermidis*. (iii) Baird-Parher classification into 6 groups based on coagulase and phosphatase, acid production from sugar, and pigment production.

# STAPHYLOCOCCUS AUREUS

## General characteristics

- Ovoid or spherical in shape, 0.8-0.9 μ in size, non motile, nonsporing, Gram positive, rarely encapsulated; usually arranged in clusters due to cell division occurring in 3 planes
- Aerobic and grows easily at optimum temperature of 37°C and pH of 7.4. In nutrient agar on 24 hour incubation produce golden yellow circular, convex, smooth 2-4 mm (pinhead), shiny and opaque colonies The pigment is a lipoprotein and its production is augmented when 1% glycerol monoacetate or milk is incorporated into the medium. Pigment production is optimum at 22°C in aerobic culture.
- In fluid media produces uniform turbidity but no pigment.
- In blood agar there in wide zone of betahaemolysis (clear zone) around the colonies; most marked on rabbit or sheep blood.
- In Mac Conkey medium colonies are small and pink.
- In egg yolk medium organisms produce opacity through action of lipolytic enzymes acting on lipovitelin of egg yolk.
- Selective media for Staphylococci include media containing 8-10% NaCl, lithium chloride, tellurite and polymyxin.

## Biochemical reactions

- Ferment glucose, lactose, sucrose, maltose and mannitol with production of acid but no gas

- Phosphatase is only produced by *Staph Aureus*. It is catalase as well as coagulase positive and liquefies gelatin
- All pathogenic strains are coagulase positive, ferment mannitol, produce betahaemolysis, liquefy gelatin. hydrolyse urea, reduce nitrates to nitrites, produce phosphatase and golden yellow pigment.
- Can withstand 60°C for 30 minutes, 1% phenol for 15 minutes but easily killed by 1% mercury perchloride
- Penicillin resistance is due to production of betalactamase which is under plasmid control.

## Antigenic structure

Staphylococci contain both antigenic polysaccharides and proteins. Peptidoglycan, a poly saccharide plays important role in pathogenicity. It elicits production of IL - 1, acts as chemoattractant for polymorphs and activates complements. Techoic acids that are polymers of glycerol or ribitol phosphate linked to cell wall peptidoglycan are antigenic. Antitechoic antibodies are particularly important in Staphylococcal endocarditis. Proetin A, a cell wall component, binds strongly to Fc portion of IgG facilitating agglutination but it may interfere with phagocytosis. Antigenic structure is of little use in identification of staphylococcus.

## Biotypes

There are six biotypes A-G. Biotype A strain is pathogenic to man and is characterized by pigments production, fibrinolysis, haemolysis, teluerite reduction etc. Phage typing is useful in epidemiological investigation of Staphylococcal infection. A set of 28 phages are usually employed.

The strains are divided into 4 groups, the human strains belong to phage group I, II, III. Hospital infections are usually due to strains belonging to group I or III.

**Staphylococcal enzymes**

- Coagulase produced by Staphylococci can be free or bound. Free coagulase is heat labile, antigenic and filterable. It has 7 antigenic types but most human strains produce A type. The enzyme has antiphagocytic action. It brings about clotting of human or rabbit plasma. Bound coagulase (clumping factor) is heat stable and it does not convert fibrinogen to fibrin. It is componert of cell wall and is liberated on autolysis of the cell.
- Phosphatase is produced by coagulase positive strains. For its demonstration, organisms are cultured on agar medium containing phenolphthalein diphosphate which when exposed to ammonia vapor shows bright pink colours due to liberation of free phenolphthalein.
- Hyaluronidase is especially produced by Staphylococci causing impetigo contagiosa.
- Deoxyribonuclease is also produced by coagulase positive staphylococci.

**Toxins**

The staphylococcal toxins include haemolysin, leucocidin, enterotoxin, fibrinolysin, exfoliative toxin, TSS toxin, scarlantina toxin, nucleases, proteases, lipases etc. 4 types of antigenically distinct staphylococcal haemolysins are known - alpha, beta, gamma and delta. Alpha haemolysin is important; since is leucocidal, cytotoxic, dermonecrotoxic and lethal. Beta haemolysin is produced by staphylococci isolated from animals; is produced both aerobically and anaerobically and is less toxic. Gamma haemolysin is the weakest. Leucocidin is a variant of alpha haemolysin with leucocidal activity. Pantovalentine is a distinct toxin toxic to polymorphs and macrophages. Enterotoxin causing diarrhoea and vomiting is a heat stable trypsin resistant protein having six antigenic types (A to F). Type A and B are most prevalent and bacteriophage group III produce it. Fibrinolysin is produced in later phases of growth. By causing lysis of fibrin it helps in dislodgement of infected intravascular thrombi leading to staphylococcal septicemia. Exfoliative toxin is implicated in staphylococcal scalded skin syndrome. Some strains of staphylococci produce toxic shock syndrome. Toxin-1 resembling enterotoxin produces fever, shock, skin rash and desquamation.

**Virulence factors**

Virulence factors important in *Staph. aureus* are (a) cell wall polysaccharide that confers rigidity and integrity (b) techoic acid that protects from complement mediated opsonization and facilitates attachment of cocci to host cell surfaces (c) protein A - that is antiphagocytic and anticomplement (d) hyaluronidase, lipase and coagulase.

**Pathogenicity**

Staphylococci cause pyogenic infections involving (a) skin - furuncle, styes, boils, carbuncle, impetigo, pemphigus (b) deeper structures - osteomyelitis, pharyngitis, tonsillitis, sinusitis, breast abscess, pulmonary abscess, endocarditis etc. Scalded skin syndrome is caused by phage group II. Toxic shock syndrome is common to tampoon users manifesting with high fever, hypotension, searlantiniform rash, cardiac and renal failure. (c) food poisoning due to preformed staphylococcal enterotoxin by contaminated meat, milk and milk products and fish.

## Laboratory diagnosis

- Gram stain of pus showing Gram positive cocci in clusters
- Culture of specimen - golden yellow colonies with beta haemolysis.
- Serological diagnosis for deeper infections e.g., antibodies to techoic acid in endocarditis.
- Methicillin resistant *Staph aureus* (MRSA) was isolated in 1960.
- Mec A gene in them encodes for a variant penicillin binding protein that has reduced affinity for beta lactam antibiotics. MRSA is responsible for more than 50% of nosocomial infections. 10-30% of staphylococci belong to MRSA.

## STREPTOCOCCUS

**General Characteristics** - Gram positive cocci arranged in chains, non motile and non spore forming.

**Classification** - (a) Morphological - pathogenic and nonpathogenic (b) Culture based - obligate anaerobes, aerobes or facultative anaerobes; alpha haemolytic (grenish discolouration around colony) and betahaemolytic (clear colourless zone) (c) Biochemical - mannitol fermenters (enterococci), non mannitol fermenter (*S. pyogenes* and *S. viridans*) (d) Antigenic - based on polysaccharide - C - hapten antigen on cell wall e.g. Lancefield group A to V. Most haemolytic streptococci that produce human infection belong to group A; commonly called *Streptococcus Pyogenes.*

## STREPTOCOCCUS PYOGENES

## General characteristics

- 0.5-1μ in diameter, arranged in chains due to division in one plane, usually encapsulated, non spore forming, non motile. The capsule is composed of hyaluronic acid.

- Aerobe/facultative anaerobe with optimum growth at 37°C, growth enhanced by addition of blood/scrum, ascitic fluid and glucose.
- Culture in fluid media shows granular growth with powdery deposit and no pellicle formation. Culture in blood agar shows 0.5-1 mm pin point circular transparent colonies with areas of haemolysis. Virulent strains produce matted colonies (granular) where as avirulent strains produce glossy colonies. Strains with capsule produce mucoid colonies.

**Biochemical characteristic**

- Ferments lactose, glucose, maltose, sorbitol producing acid but no gas. It is catalase negative, does not liquefy gelatin
- Easily destroyed by heat, resistant to crystal violet but highly sensitive to bacitracin.

**Antigenic properties**

- Haemolytic streptococci possess a group specific polysaccharide C and three type specific protein antigen M, T and R and nucleoproteins
- Polysaccharide C antigen confers serological specificity and classifies them into 20 Lance field groups. Human strain belongs to group A. The antigen is integrated into cell wall and can be extracted by HCl, formamide, autoclaving etc.
- M antigen acts as virulence factor and antibody to it is protective. The antigen inhibits phagocytosis. Antibodies against T antigen are not protective. Both R and T antigen are not related to virulence.

**Toxins**

- Haemolysins consisting of (a) streptolysin O, a heat labile strongly antigenic cardiotoxic protein (b) streptolysis S, non antigenic, often nephrotoxic
- Erythrogenic toxin incriminated in scarlet fever, produced when infected by bacteriophage
- Streptokinase (fibrinolysin) produced by strains of A, C and G
- Deoxy ribo nuclease (streptodornase) liquefies pus by depolymerizing DNA.
- Diphosphopyricine nucleotidase (DPNase), believed to be leucotoxic
- Hyaluronidase - the spreading factor, typically produced by M type 4, 22 which have no capsule
- Protease - an intracellular enzyme whose biological significance in not known.

| *Group* | *Disease* |
|---|---|
| A | Majority of human streptococcal disease |
| B | Sepsis in newborn, puerperal infection |
| C | Mild respiratory infection |
| D | Endocarditis, urogenital infections, wound infections |
| E | Diseases of pigs and cows |
| F | Respiratory infection, endocarditis |
| G | Mild respiratory infection |
| H, K | Endocarditis |
| L, M, N | Genital tract infections in dogs |
| O | Endocarditis |
| P - V | Unknown |

**Clinical spectrum**

- Respiratory infection - tonsillitis, pharyngitis, otitis media, Ludwig's angina

- Skin infections - lymphangitis, cellulitis, carbuncle, scarlet fever
- Puerperal sepsis, septicemia, pyemia
- Non suppurative complications - acute rheumatic fever and acute glomerulonephritis

Acute rheumatic fever is characteried by fever, pancarditis, migratory polyarthritis, some times chorea and subcutaneous nodule and usually follows pharyngo-tonsillitis. It is due to hypersensitivity to streptococcal protein; reactivation occuring with reinfection. Acute glomerulonephritis is by group A (4, 2, 12, 49, 52, 57); type 12 being most common. Besides sore throat skin infection can also produce it. Unlike carditis recurrence or progression are unlikely (hence penicillin prophylaxis not necessary)

**Laboratory Diagnosis**

- Leucocytosis, rise in PMN cells, raised ESR and CRP
- Gram positive cocci arranged in chains in Gram stain of infected specimen (sputum, throat swab, CSF etc.)
- Typical colonics with betahaemolysis in culture. For rapid diagnosis swab or pus are cultured in broth and after 2-3 hours smears are stained with fluorescein labelled group A antiserum
- Antistreptolysin 'O' titre (ASO litre) - Value above 200 in adults and 300 units in children indicates streptococcal infection
- Dick test can find out susceptibility to scarlet fever. 0.2 ml of erythrogenic toxin is injected intradermally on the forearm and same amount of inactivated toxin on the other forearm as control. A positive reaction i.e. appearance of red rash within six hours means no immunity to scarlet fever.

- Schultz - Charlton reaction - Erythrogenic toxin is injected intradermally in a patient with scarlantinal rash. There is local blanching of the rash

## Group B Streptococci

*Streptococcus agalactiae* causes mastitis in cows. It is often a commeasal in human throat and vagina. Some times it may cause septicemia, endocarditis, puerperal infection and meningitis.

## Group C Streptococci

*Streptococcus equisimilis* is often isolated from purperal infection, cellulitis, and scarlet fever. It produces streptolysin and fibrinolysin.

## Group D Streptococci

This group includes enterococci like *Enterococcus faecalis, Enterococcus faecium, Enterococcus durans. Enterococcus avium etc. Enterococcus faecalis* is the most common. It ferments mannitol with production of gas. It can be grown on blood tellurite producing black colonies.

### *Characteristics*

- Form normal flora of vagina and lower Gl tract
- Can grow in 6.5% NaCl, 40% bile, at 45°C, at pH 9.6
- In sheep blood agar can cause alpha, beta haemolysis or may be non haemolytic.
- In Mac Conkey medium form tiny deep pink colonies.
- Are non motile, Gram positive, non capsulated arranged in pairs or short chains
- Survive in 60°C upto 30 minutes.

- Show uniform turbidity in fluid culture media but in blood agar form circular raised low convex colonies.
- Can produce cystitis, pyelitis, cervicitis, puerperal infection and subacute bacterial endocarditis, peritonitis, biliary infection.
- Non enterococci in group D are *Streptococcus equinus, Streptococcus bovis, Streptococcus avium,* often commensal in throat; can cause septicemia, endocarditis, urinary tract infection but unlike enterococci are susceptible to penicillin.

**Alphahaemolytic Streptococci**

This group includes *Streptococcus viridans, Streptococcus salivarium, Streptococcus nitis, Streptococcus MG etc. Streptococcus viridans* is the commensal of oral flora, on blood agar it produces alpha haemolysis and has five species - *S. salivarium, S nutans, S. sanguis, S milleri and S. mitior*. Most are normally nonpathogenic.

Flesh eating streptococci are virulent strains that act by liberating toxin and deprive cells of oxygen. They have claimed many lives in the West.

## PNEUMOCOCCUS

**General characteristics**

- Gram positive, encapsulated lanceolate diplococci, nonmotile, nonsporing, flame shaped, 1μ in size. The capsule encloses each pair. In India ink preparation the capsule appears as a clear halo.
- Requires serum or whole blood for growth; grows best at 37°C at pH 7.6 in presence of 5-10% $CO_2$.
- In blood agar the colonies are small (0.5-1 mm), dome shaped with alphahaemolysis around (green-

ish discolouration), uniform turbidity in liquid medium.

- Catalase and oxidase negative, ferment sugar and inulin with production of acid but no gas.
- Readily destroyed by heat, phenol, potassium permanganate and antiseptics
- Antigens possessed are - nucleoproteins, species specific polysaccharide hepten and capsular poly saccharide.
- Capsular poly saccharide determines type specificity of the organism and its virulence. 90 types of pneumococci are known
- Typing may be carried out by (i) agglutination of cocci with type specific antiserum (ii) precipitation of capsular polysaccharide with specific sera (iii) capsular swelling reaction (Quellong reaction)
- The capsular polysaccharide protects the organism from phagocytosis
- Pneumococci attach to nasopharyngeal mucosa through their surface antigen A or choline binding proteins. They produce no toxin except leucocidin.
- In humans 80% cases lobar pneumonia and 60% of bronchopneumonia are caused by pneumococci. Sinusitis, meningitis, otitis media, peritonitis, empyema are also caused by them.

## Laboratory diagnosis

- Poly morphonuclear leucocytosis
- Gram positive flame shapped diplococci in smear of specimen
- Flat umbonated colonies with alphahaemolysis in blood agar; can be differentiated from *Strepto Coc-*

*cus viridans* by inulin fermentation, bile solubility and optochin sensitivity tests

- Immunologic diagnosis by detection of pneumecoccal capsular polysaccharide through latex agglutination and counter immuno electro phoresis. However due to cross reaction this method is less specific.
- Mice innoculation to show diplococci in heart blood and peritoneal fluid is a very rapid diagnostic tool.
- Immunological protection available with heptavalent pneumococcal conjugate vaccine recommended for children of 2-23 months. Pneumococcal polysaccharide vaccine is recommuded in high risk groups (asplenia, sickle cell disease, lymphomà, leukemia, cardiorespiratory disease, cirrhosis, nephrosis, HIV etc.)
- Efficiency in immunocompetent is 60-70%; but only 10% in severly immunocompromised.

## NEISSERIA

Neisseria are gram negative, aerobic, nonspore forming nonmotile oxidase positive cocci arranged in pairs. The genus has 30 species of which *N. meningitidis* and *N. gonorrhoea* are important pathogens to humans.

### NEISSERIA MENINGITIDIS

#### General characteristics

- Gram negtive, oval or spherical 0.6-0.8 μ in size, arranged in pairs with adjacent sides flattened; often have microcapsule and are intracellular in clinical specimens.
- Grow well in media enriched with blood, serum

or ascitic fluid especially in pressence of 10% $CO_2$. In fluid media form mild to moderate turbidity. Colonies in solid media are moist, smooth, elevated, round, convex and translucent without haemolysis

- Catalase and oxidase positive, ferment glucose and maltose producing acid but no gas.
- 13 sero subgroups of meningococci exist (A, B, C, D, X, Y, Z, W-135, 29E, H, I: K, L) based on immunologic specificity of capsular polysaccharides.
- The nucleoproteins (P. substance) of meningococci have some toxic effects.
- Highly susceptible to heat, descication, pH variation and disinfectants.
- Colonize nasopharynx and spread to CNS to cause purulent meningitis; meningococcal septicemia is favoured by complement deficiency
- Meningococcemia presents with acute fever, chill, cutaneous rash, petechial haemorrhages, often with metastatic involvement of joint, ear, lungs, myocardium, and adrenal; endotoxin released from lysed organisms produce haemorrhagic manifestations.

**Laboratory diagnosis**

- Polymorponuclear leucocytosis
- Turbid CSF with plenty of puscells, some containing gram positive intracellular diplococci. Typical colonies in blood agar.
- Blood culture positive in early disease.
- Positive antibody titre to meningococci in convalescent sera.
- Immunological protection available—monvalent (group A or C); bivalent (group A and C) and

quadrivalent (A, C, Y, W135), single dose of 50 mg SC for adults and two doses at 3 month interval for children; protective efficacy 90%.

## NEISSERIA GONORRHOAE

### General characteristics

- Gram negative, oval or spherical (0.6-0.8μ) bean shaped diplococci, usually intracellular (within PMN leucocytes)
- Grow well in enriched media like chocolate agar at 37°C; translucent, gray white colonies of 0.5-1 mm with glistening surface and entire margin. Consistency is viscid and difficult to emulsify.
- Growth on serum broth is poor with no turbidity
- Thayer Martin medium containing vancomycin, colistin and nystatin is the selective medium for *N. gonorrohoea* that inhibits contaminants and nonpathogenic neisseria
- Catalase and oxidase positive; ferments glucose with formation of acid but no gas.
- Classified into 4 biotypes ($T_1$, $T_2$, $T_3$, $T_4$) depending upon colony morphology, auto agglutinability and virulence. $T_1$ and $T_2$ are virulent, not $T_2$ and $T_4$.
- Antigenically heterogenous, possess polysaccharides and nucleoproetins; have a capsule demonstrated by negative staining.
- Easily killed by heat, drying and antiseptics.
- Strictly human parasite producing gonorrhoea manifesting in (a) men with urethritis, prostatitis, seminal vesiculitis, epididymitis (b) in women with vaginitis, bartholinitis, endometritis, salpingitis. Proctitis occurs in both sexes. Gonococcal septicemia can lead to septic arthritis, ulcerative en-

docarditis etc. Ophthalmia neonatorum occurs from contract of infection from mother's birth passage.

- Attach to surface epithelial cells by pili and protein II and often secrete protease to destroy surface IgA in mucosa.
- Produce iron repressible protein (FeRPS) that remove iron from trasferrin and lactoferrin.
- Secrete several proteinases, peptidases and phospholipases.

**Laboratory diagnosis**

- Raised ESR and polymorphonuclear leukocytosis
- Gram stain of purulent discharge from urethra/ vagina show intracellular gram negative diplococci.
- Fluorescent antibody technique is specific and sensitive but detection of antibodies against gonococal pili, outer membrane protein and lipopolysaccharide by flocculation/complement fixation test are less sensitive
- Nucleic acid probe may diagnose presence of gonococci in urethral and vaginal specimens.
- Immunoprotection with gonococcal pilus vaccine or lipopolysaccharide is possible but not reliable.

**Table 8.2 : Differences between gonococci and meningococci**

| Meningococci | Gonococci |
|---|---|
| Adjacent sides are flat | Adjacent sides concave |
| Colonies are butyrous, easily emulsified | Viscid colonies difficult to emulsify |
| Ferment glucose and maltose | Ferment only glucose |

Commensal neisseriae inhabiting the respiratory tract are *N. catarrhalis, N. flavescens* and *N. sicca*. They all grow well on nutrient agar at 27°C. Only *N. sicca* ferments glucose and maltose. *N. flavescens* produces pigmented yellow colonies. *N. sicca* - opaque, wrinkled colonies and *N. catarrhalis* - translucent, opaque colonies Veillonella are anaerobic gram negative cocci of normal oral flora and are nonpathogenic.

## CORYNEBACTERIA

They are gram positive non acid fast and non motile bacilli occuring in palisade and having club shaped swelling at both ends. Staining is irregular. Corynebacterium diphtheriae is the commonly encountered human pathogen.

## CORYNEBACTERIUM DIPHTHERIAE

**General characteristics**

- Thin slender rod, 3-6 μ long with clubbing at one or both ends. Nonmotile, non spore forming, have metachromatic granules (Babes Ernst granule), stained dark purple with methylene blue. The granules consist of polymerized metaphosphate.
- Arrangement of bacilli is in V or L pattern (Chineese letter pattern) due to incomplete separation after division.
- Are acrobe and facultative anaerobe, growing well at pH 7.2, at 37°C in enriched media containing blood, serum or egg.
- In serum broth grow with formation of pellicles and turbidity
- In Loeffler's slope show abundant growth after 6 hours, the colonies being small, granular, moist, creamy, and glistening with irregular edges.

- Blood tellurite medium (0.04%) can identify corynebacteria to gravis, mitis and intermedia from degree of reduction of tellurite to its metallic form forming gray to black colonies.
- Ferment glucose and maltose with acid production; starch and glycogen are only fermented by gravis.
- Catalase positive, oxidase negative, do not liquefy gelatin and indole negative.
- Readily destroyed by heat but resistant to drying.
- Antigenically heterogenous; gravis has 13 types; mitis 40 and intermedius 4.
- About 40 bacteriophage types exist; type I & III are mitis; IV to VI intermedius; VII avirulent gravis and rest virulent gravis.
- Produce powerful exotoxin consisting of factors A and B; A is lethal factor and B is spreading factor; toxin production is related to presence of beta-phage, presence of optimum concentration of iron in the medium (0.1 mg/ml), pH and osmotic pressure.
- Do not actively invade deep tissues, nor produce septicemia; site of infection localized to nasopharynx, tonsils, larynx conjunctiva, vulva, vagina, skin around mouth and nose; causing death due to asphyxia, acute circulatory failure. Post diphtheritic palsy of palate occurs in 3rd week, myocarditis etc can occur but with spontaneous recovery.
- Diagnosis is from smear examination showing gram positive thin bacilli in Chineese letter pattern. Culture be made in Loeffler's slope, blood tellurite or blood agar for characteristic colonies. Albert stain demonstrates metachromatic granules.
- Virulence test can be done *Invivo* (intradermal) or *Invitro* (Elek test). In invivo test two guinea pigs

are injected with diphtheria culture, one of them protected with 500 units diphtheria antitoxin. If organism is virulent the unprotected guinea pig dies within 4 days. In Elek's test (gel precipitation test) the line of precipitation occurs at the meeting of toxin and antitoxin on the growth plate.

- Individual susceptibility is tested with Shick test; persons without previous exposure to diphtheria or its toxoid develop rash at the site of toxin injection but not those with protective immunity. A pseudoreaction is erythema within 6-24 hours, disappearing completely within 4 days occurring in toxin injected as well as control arm injected with inactivated toxin, indicating hypersensitiveness.
- **Diphtheroids** are nonpathogenic diphtheria like organisms found on conjunctiva, nasopharynx, oral cavity and genitalia. *C. hominis* is part of oral flora and *C. xerosis* of skin. *Propionibacterium acne* is anaerobic, splits fatty acids in sebaceous secretions producing inflammatory response of acne. Diphtheroids are short, stumpy with parallel sides and rounded ends. They do not exhibit pleomorphism and have no metachromatic granules. Unlike *C. diphtheriae* they grow in ordinary media, ferment sucrose in addition to glucose and are avirulent.

  Corynebacterium genus is currently divided into three groups or species :

(1) The nonlipophilic fermentative ones including: *C.diphtheriae, C. xerosis, C. striatum* etc.

(2) Non lipophilic non fermentative : *C. pseudodiphtheriticum.*

(3) *Lipophilic : C.jeekeium*, *C. urealyticum. C. jeikeium*

causes infections in immuno compromised and *C. urealyticum* causes pyelonephritis. Some strains of *C. ulcerans* and *C. pseudotuberculosis* can produce diphtheria toxin.

**Table 8.3 : Differentiation of Corynebacterium diphtheriae**

| *Gravis* | *Intermedius* | *Mitis* |
|---|---|---|
| Short, uniformly stained, few granules | Long, irregularly stained, no granules | Long, curved, prominent granules |
| Colony - greyish, black centre, semitranslucent periphery | Colony - dull, granular centre, smooth glistening periphery | Colony is shiny black |
| Variable haemolysis | Non haemolytic | Haemolytic |
| In broth culture granular deposit, no turbidity | Clearing turbidity granular deposit | Diffuse turbidity |
| Glycogen and starch fermentation | No fermentation | No fermentation |

## CLOSTRIDIA

Clostridia are Gram positive, anaerobic, spore forming, spindle shaped and highly pleormorphic bacilli. They are motile with peritrichate flagella except *C. perfringens. C. welchii* and *C. butyricum* are encapsulated.

## CLOSTRIDIUM TETANI

### General Characteristics

- It is long slendere (5 μ) occurring singly or in chains, motile and nonencapsulated. Spores are spherical, terminal and bulging giving the bacilli drum stick appearance.
- Obligatory anaerobe, growing only in absence of

oxygen, lack cytochrome oxidase, catalase, peroxidase and superoxide dismutase, grow fairly well in ordinary media like nutrient agar, cooked meat, blood agar and lactose yolk milk medium. In nutrient agar produce irregular round, greyish yellow translucent colonies with granular surface and ill defined edges.

- Grow well in cooked meat with turbidity and gas formation.
- Does not ferment any sugar, does not coagulate milk, forms indole, minimal proteolysis.
- Spores can survive in soil for years; autoclaving at 120°C for 20 minutes kills spores but can withstand boilling upto 90 minutes. 4% iodine or $H_2O_2$ kill spores effectively.
- Produce 3 toxins - tetanospasmin (neurotoxin), haemolysin and nonspasmogenic peripherally acting neurotoxin. Tetanospasmin is heat labile protein of molecular weight 67,000; acts like strychnine inhibiting synthesis and liberation of acetylcholine. Orally ingested toxin is digested and hence ineffective.
- Wound with soil contamination, availability of necrosed tissue, ionisable calcium salts, lactic acid and co infection with pyogenic organisms enhance clostridial growth and toxin production.
- Tetanospasmin produces tetanus - local or generalised. Tetanus neonatorum occurs from infection of umbilical stump; post abortal and puerperal tetanus occurs due to improper aseptic measures; splanchnic tetanus involves muscles of deglutition and respiration; in cephalic tetanus there is involvement of facial muscles. Trismus is first sign of tetanus with increased salivation.

- Laboratory diagnosis is from Gram stain and culture; animal inoculation.
- Active immunisation is by tetanus toxoid 1 ml IM 3 doses at 0, 1, 6 months that confers immunity for 10 years. Passive immunization is with human ATS (300 units) or horse ATS (3000 units) with half lives of 3 weeks and 2 days respectively.

## CLOSTRIDIUM PERFRINGENS (CLOSTRIDIUM WELCHII)

### General Characteristics

- It is normaly present in human and animal large intestine; hence found in feces and contaminates perineum and buttocks.
- Gram positive anaerobe with straight parallel sides, rounded or truncated ends, occurring singly or in chains; spores are central or subterminal; nonmotile, encapsulated.
- Fairly good growth in cooked meat medium forming turbidity with production of gas.
- In nutrient agar two types of colonies appear (1) 2-4 mm round, smooth, butyrous emulsifiable colonies (2) umbonate colonies with brownish opaque centre and crenated edges.
- Ferment glucose, maltose, lactose and sucrose with production of acid and gas but no indole.
- Spores are resistant to antiseptics and disinfectants in common use but die in autoclaving at 120°C for 20 minutes.
- Antigenically are of 6 types - (A-E), produce atleast 12 types of toxins, the major 4 being alpha, beta, epsilon and iota. Alpha toxin is more potent, necorolytic, haemolytic and lethal. It has lecithi-

nase activity and gives positive Nagler's reaction which is neutralised by antialpha toxin.

- Only type A and F are pathogenic; type A producing gas gangrene and food poisoning. Besides *C. welchii* gas gangrene is also produced by *C. septium. C. edematicus* and anaerobic streptococci.
- Anaerobic myositis is the most serious form of clostridial wound infection; the exotoxin producing toxemia, wound edema, haemolysis, myonecrosis.
- F strains produce necrotising enteritis.
- *C. perfringens* is also implicated in gangrenous appendicitis, biliary tract disease, brain abscess, urogenital infection.
- Diagnosis is from Gram stain of smear, anerobic culture and identification from Nagler's reaction, biochemical reactions and animal innoculation studies.
- In clostridial food poisoning the stool smear shows abundance of anaerobic, nonmotile, nonhaemolytic gram positve bacilli.

## Clostridium botulinum

- Gram positive, anaerobic, nonencapsulated with terminal oval bulging spores; motile due to peri trichate flagella; can occur singly, in pairs and chains.
- Toxigenically are of 6 types (A to F), cultural characterstics also differ from one to another.
  In nutrient a gas produce irrugar glistering butyrous colonies with granular surface.
- Spore is highly resistant surviving at 100°C for several hours.

- Ferment glucose and maltose with production of acid and gas.
- The exotoxin is most lethal neuro toxin known inhibiting release of acetylcholine at neuromuscular juntion leading to flaccid palsy. The toxin is stable, resists digestion and gets absorbed into blood stream from intestine.
- Botulinum toxin is now used in treatment of blepharospasm, torticolis, spasticity, strabismus, motor disorders of esophagus, migraine, injection of spastic sphincters, facial cosmesis, laryngeal muscle spasm.
- *C. botulinium* is noninvasive, botulism occurring due to ingestion of preformed toxins in caned food, meat.Human botulism is caused by type A, B and E.
- Diagnosis is based on demonstration of bacillus or toxin in food or feces.
- Active immunization with toxoid is effective; trivalent antitoxin given IV early is life shaving.

### Clostridium Difficile

- Gram negative anaerobic rod with bipolar sporing giving dumb bell appearance.
- Produce necrotizing glycoprotein toxin to cause haemorrhagic fulminant colitis.
- Stool culture in brain heart infusion agar (BHIA) in presence of 10% $CO_2$, 10% $H_2$ and 80% $N_2$ yields the organism.

## ENTEROBACTERIACEAE

They comprise numerous interrelated gram negative bacilli, some motile with peritrichate flagella, nonsporing, fermentig glucose with or without formation of gas, reducing nitrates into nitrites; some are anaerobic.

## Classification

(i) Lactose fermentation (a) Early lactose fermenter - e.g. *E-coli*, Klebsiella (b) Late lactose fermenter - *Shigella soni* (c) Non lactose fermenter - Salmonella

(ii) Based on cultural and biochemical properties - Classified into 5 tribes :

Tribe I - Escherichia, Salmonella, Shigella, Citrobacter

Tribe II - Klebsiella, Enterobacter, Serratia, Hafnia

Tribe III - Proteus

Tribe IV - Erwinia

Tribe V - Yersenia

(pestis, enterocolitica, pseudotuberculosis)

## *ESCHERICHIA COLI*

### *General Characteristics*

- Gram negative non encapsulated, short, plump, motile non spore forming.
- Aerobe and facultative anaerobe; growing on liquid broth with uniform turbidity.
- Form smooth circular colourless, butyrous colonies on nutrient agar; colonies are pink on MacConkey medium due to lactose fermentation, some strains cause betahaemolysis in blood agar.
- Ferment lactose, sucrose, maltose, glucose and mannitol forming acid and gas; positive for indole and methyl red, don't produce $H_2S$; don't produce urease
- Have 4 types of antigens — (i) somatic or O antigen (ii) surface or K antigen (iii) flagellar or H an-

tigen (iv) fimbrial or F antigen. 175 types of O artigen, 160 types of K antigen, 75 types of H antigen are known.

- Produce endotoxin and two types of exotoxin (a) enterotoxin - heat stable and heat labile forms (b) haemolysin
- Production of enterotoxin is regulated by plasmids. Enterotoxin producing strains belong to group 0 (26, 55 III etc.) but normal colon strains belong to 0-1, 2, 4, 8 etc.
- Enteropathogenic *E.coli* (EPEC) carry B type K antigen and cause diarrhoea in babies. Enterotoxigenic *E. coli* (ETEC) cause diarohoea in children as well as travellers. Entero invasive *E. coli* (EIEC) produce dysentery due to nucosal invasion. They invade HELA cells in tissue culture - Entero haemorhagic *E.coli* (EHEC) produce verotoxin to cause haemorrhagic colitis.
- *E.coli* serotypes causing urinary tract infection are 1, 2, 4, 6, 7 strains of 0 type. Strains carrying K antigens cause pyelonephritis while strains causing cystitis lack K antigen. *E.coli* strains can be differentiated by (a) electron microscopy for detection of fimbriae (b) uroepithelial adhesion assay (c) haemagglutination test (d) salt aggregation test (h) haemolysin production (f) colcinogeny (g) aerobactin production (h) dulcitol fermentation
- *E.coli* also cause wound infection, peritonitis, cholecystitis, meningitis etc, so also septicemia.
- Diagnosis is based on culture of urine, stool, pus in blood agar or Mac Conkey plate showing indole position, MR positive, VP and citrate negative lactose fermenting, gram negative motile organisms.

***Serratia infection*** : *S. marcescens* causes majority of serratia infections with involvement of respiratory and genito urinary system, surgical wounds. They are lactose negative and some of the strains are red-pigmented.

***Citrobacter infections*** : are caused by *C. freundii, C. koseri* which primarily infect urinary tract, can cause meningitis and brain abscess particularly in immunocompromised.

*Moragnella morgagni and Providentia rettgeri* cause urinary infections in patients on indwelling catheters, site infections, ventilator associated pneumonia, and intraabdominal infections. They are non lactose fermenters. *Edwardsiella tarda* shares features with salmonella species and *Vibrio vulnificus.* It causes diarrhoea. Other gram negative bacteria from genera *Hafnia*, *Cedecea*, *Pantoea* and *Ewingella* are opportunistic pathogens.

## SALMONELLA

- Gram negative, motile, non encapsulated, nonsporing rods of 2-4 μ long
- Aerobe and facultative anaerobe, grow at pH of 6-8 forming uniform turbidity in broth but no pellicle formation. In blood agar colonies are large (2-3 mm) circular, low convex, translucent, smooth, non haemolytic.
- Jet black colonies with metallic sheen due to $H_2S$ production in Wilson and Blair bismuth sulphite medium; colourless in MacConkey and desoxy cholate citrate medium.
- All salmonella ferment glucose, maltose and mannitol forming acid and gas except for *Salmonella typhi* which only produces acid but no gas. MR

positive, VP negative; do not produce indole/$H_2S$/urease.

- Easily killed by heating, pasturization, chlorination
- Have (a) somatic (o) antigen, a phospholipid protein polysaccharide complex (b) a highly immunogenic flagellar antigen (H) (c) Vi antigen. Unlike O antigen H antigen is strongly immunogenic; O agglutination occurs slowly. O antigen classfies salmonella into 65 serogroups.
- Antigenic and phase variation is common to salmonella. Smooth to rough (S to R) variation leads to loss of O antigen and virulence.
- Phage typing helpful when serological and biochemical differentiation of salmonella is difficult. *S. typhi* with Vi antigen can have 106 phage types.
- Salmonella cause enteric fever *(S. typhi)*, paratyphoid *(S. paratyphi)* and food poisoning (*S. typhimurium, S. enteritidis*). Septicemia is caused by *S. choleraesuis*
- Diagnosis is based on blood culture, clot culture, stool culture. urine culture, bone marrow culture. Bile culture is important for detection of carrier.
- Serological diagnosis is based on Widal test that measures H and O antibodies. H agglutination leads to formation of cotton wooly clump and O agglutination is seen as matted granular irragular disc like pattern. Hence conical bottom tube (Dreyer's) is used for H agglutination and round bottomed tube (Felix) for O agglutination. O titre above 1:80 and H titre above 1:200 indicate positive Widal test.

- Immunoprophylaxis is with oral Ty 21 a mutant *S. typhi* strain lacking CIDP galactose 4 epimerase.

## PSEUDOMONAS

- They are mostly saprophytes being found in water, soil, and on decomposed matter; hence are secondary invaders. *Pseudomonas aeruginosa* is the prominent member of this group
- The organism is slender, aerobic non encapsulated gram negative, actively motile with polar flagella.
- Produce dense turbidity and surface pellicle on broth culture; large irregular opaque colonies on nutrient agar giving musty or earthy smell or firuity odor due to production of aminoacetophenone from tryptophane.
- Most strains produce pigments like pyocyanin (bluish green), fluroscein (yellowish green), proverdin (green), pyorubin (red) and pyomelanin (black)
- Produce nonlactose fermenting colonies in MacConkey medium; beta haemolysis on blood agar.
- Somatic 'O' antigen divides *P. aeruginosa* into 17 serogroups; sero group 6 and 11 are responsible for nosocomial infections.
- Flagellar and fimbrial antigens are present so also plasma membrane antigens.
- About 105 pyocin types of *Pseudomonas aeruginosa* are known.
- Ferment glucose to produce acid only; reduce nitrate to nitrite; are catalase and oxidase positive.
- Mostly resistant to common antiseptics and disinfectant and most antibiotics except polymyxin, colistin, third generation cephalosporins

- Toxins produced include lecithinase, proteinase, elastage, creatinase, exotoxin (A, S, cytolysin) endotoxin and haemolysin
- Produce nosocomial infections, secondary infection of would, burn, chronic ulcer; can cause septicemia, urinary tract infection, empyema, brain abscess, endocarditis, eye and ear infections, burn and joint infections.
- Diagnosis is based on observation of greenish pus with sweetish odor from lesion; greenish blue colonies in nutrient agar.

*Burkholderia cepacia like P. aeruginosa* is primarily an opportunistic pathogen causing pneumonia, meningitis, endocarditis, urinary tract infections nad wound infections. It causes fluminant respiratory infections in patients of cystic fibrosis.

***Stenotrophomonas maltophila*** causes pneumonia and other infections akin to *B. cepacia. B pscudomallei* causes melioidosis charactercised by pneumonitis often with septicemia.

Other pseudomonas species involved in human disease are *P. fluorescens, P.putida*, *B. picketti*, *B. gladioli* etc.

## SHIGELLA

- Found exclusively in Gl tract of human beings
- Gram negative, aerobic, non encapsulated, non motile rods.
- Form small circular, convex, smooth, translucent colonies on nutrient agar.
- Excepting *Shigella soni* others are non lactose fermentor; lactose fermentors produce pink colonies on MacConkey agar.

- Desoxycholate citrate agar (DCA) is a selective medium for Shigella.
- Boiling, pasteurization and chlorination kill the organism but in water and ice oranism can survive upto 6 months.
- All Shigella ferment glucose with formation of acid but no gas, *Shigella sonnei* ferments mannitol and lactose, *Shigella flexneri* and *S. boydii* only mannitol where as some *Shigella dysenteriae* strains ferment indole but not mannitol and lactose.
- All are MR positive, reduce nitrate to nitrites, do not form $H_2S$, most are catalase positive; urease, citrate and KCN negative.
- Possess one or more major antigens and large number of minor somatic antigens.
- Produce enterotoxin as well as endotoxin
- *Shigella dysenteriae* has 10 serotypes, *Shigella flexneri* 10 serotypes, *Shigella boydii* 18 serotypes and *Shigella sonnei* 17 Serotypes (based on production of specific colicine). *Shigella shigae* produces most severe bacillary dysentery.
- Infecting dose is $10^3$ organisms; invade intestinal mucosa with necrosis, superficial ulceration pseudomembrane formation.
- *Shigella dysenteriae* type I infection is often complicated with arthritis, toxic neuritis, conjunctivitis, parotitis, myocarditis
- Laboratory diagnosis is based on fecal culture in MacConky and DCA media.

## VIBRIO

- They are thin, curved, Gram negative actively motile comma shaped bacilli with pollar flagella.

- Are non lactose fermenting, grow in alkaline pH, ferment glucose with production of acid only, are oxidase positive and produce indole.
- Main pathogenic members are *Vibrio cholerae*, *Vibrio eltor*, *Vibrio parahaemolyticus*, and non-agglutinable vibrio (NAV)
- *Vibrio choleriae* is a short, curved, comma shaped Gram negative bacillus occuring singly or as 'S' shaped semicircular pairs. It is actively mobile with single flagellum (darting motility).
- Grows well at alkaline pH (7.5-9.5) at 37°C. Rapid growth occurs in alkaline peptone water with formation of thick surface pellicles.
- In nutrient agar colonies are round, moist and translucent; in blood agar colonies have green colouration around them; in MacConkey agar colonies are colourless.
- Special media for *V. cholerae* include Venkat Raman media, containing 5 gm peptone and 20% salt and Cary Blair medium containing NaCl, sodium thioglycolate, sodium phosphate and calcium chloride at pH 8.4. They keep vibrios viable for months without multiplication.
- Enriched media for vibrio include alkaline peptone water at pH 8.6 end Monsur's taurocholate-tellurite peptone water at pH 9.2; plating media include alkaline bile salt agar at pH 8.2; Monsur's gelatin - taurocholate - trypticase - tellurite agar (GTTA) and thiosulphate - bromothymol blue and sucrose (TCBS).
- Vibrios ferment glucose, sucrose, maltose and mannitol with production of acid but no gas; reduce nitrate, liquefy gelatin, are oxidase positive and urease negative.

- Cholera red reaction is addition of few drops of $H_2SO_4$ to *Vibrios cholerae* growth in peptone water which gives red colour due to formation of nitrosoindole.
- Easily killed by dry/moist heat, gastric pH.
- Have O antigen and flagellar antigen. Based on O antigen 60 groups are identified.
- *V. cholerae* is divided into Inaba, Ogawa and Hikojima based on 'O' artigen subgroups with AC, AB and ABC respectively.
- Based on phage typing 5 strains of *V. cholerae* are identified.
- Cholera exotoxin (molecular weight 80,000) has A subunit and B subunit. Ganglioside $GM_1$ serves as mucosal receptor for B subunit and facilitates entry of A subunit into intestinal epithelium that activates adenyl cyclase with prolonged secretion of water and electrolytes. Cholera endotoxin has undefined role.
- Diagnosis is based on Gram stain of stool, or its hanging drop preparation showing darting motility; culture of stool in appropriate medium for oxidase positive, nitrate reduction positive, and indole positive colonies fermenting glucose, arabinose and mannose with formation of acid, but no gas.
- Agglutination with antisera can ideatify it into Inaba, Ogawa or Hikojima subtypes.
- Serological diagnosis is of limited use. Antitoxin assay, indirect haemagglutination and vibriocidal tests are available.
- Immunoprophylaxis is with killed organisms (Inaba and Ogawa) given IM with 40-60% protection lasting upto 1 year. Live mutant strain vac-

cine, streptomycin resistant and B subunit toxoid provide 80-85% protection. *V. eltor* vaccine provides 90-100% protection for upto 3 years.

- *Vibrio eltor* has caused epidemics of cholera in South East Asia with susceptibility for A, B and AB blood groups. The organism unlike *V. cholerae* causes haemolysis and agglutinates chick erythrocytes; is resistant to polymyxin B.
- Non agglutinable vibrios include *Vibrio minicus* and *Vibrio fluvialis* which cause cholera like illness.
- *Aeromonas hydrophilia* and *Plesiomonas shigelloides* also cause diarrhoeal disease and resemble *V. cholerae* morphologically. They can be differentiated by their ability to utilize aminoacids.

## CAMPYLOBACTER

- Gram negative bacilli with tapering ends, comma shaped, non motile, nonsporing
- Microaerophilic, non proteolytic, oxidase positive, reduce nitrate, don't ferment carbohydrate, indole negative.
- Produce heat labile enterotoxin that through adenyl cyclase stimulates cAMP and hence cause watery diarrhea.
- Growth is best in presence of 3-6% $O_2$, 10% $CO_2$, forming flat colonies with irregular edge.
- Have H and O antigens
- *Campylobacter jejuni* is motile with single flagellum. It grows best in selective media containing cephalothin, TMP, vancomycin or polymyxin B. The colonies are round and convex, colourless or grey. It is oxidase negative. Diagnosis is based on discovery in stool of gram negative gull wing

shaped rods with darting motility in dark field phage contrast microscopy; culture and biochemical reactions are confirmatory.

## *HELIOBACTOR PYLORI*

- Though previously named as *Campylobacter pylori* now renamed as *Heliobacter pylori* because of (a) bear multiple unipolar flagella with terminal bulbs (b) produces urease (c) different cell wall fatty acid composition and ribosomal RNA.
- Actively motile, non spore forming, curved gram negative rod.
- Microaerophilic (10% $CO_2$) with optimum growth at 37°C at pH of 6.8.
- The organism has virulence factors like vacuolating cytotoxin (VacA) and Cag Pal.
- In blood agar form circular. cloudy, glistening colonies with butyrous consistency. Grow also well in Brewer's sodium thioglycolate, Sirrow medium, Butzler medium.
- Biochemically catalase positive, urease positive, alkaline phosphatase positive and hippurate test negative.
- Hypochlorhydria favours colonization in stomach producing antral gastritis, non ulcer dyspepsia, duodenitis, submucosal gastric lymphoma and even gastric malignancy.
- Diagnosis is based on (a) discovery of organisms in gastric aspirate (b) positive urease breath test
- Produce protease, cytotoxin factors in addition to urease. Urease breaks down urea to ammonia and $CO_2$. The ammonia is directly toxic to mucosa.

## YERSENIA ENTEROCOLITICA

- A gram negative aerobic, motile bacillus, urease positive but oxidase negative
- Can be cultured on peptone agar, blood agar MacConkey deoxycholate agar; non lactose fermenter
- There are 20 serotypes; $O_3$, $O_8$, $O_9$ causing human disease
- Produce heat stable enterotoxin causing bloody diarrhoea; erythema nodosum and arthritis may follow. (Reiter syndrome)

## HAEMOPHILUS

- Small, non motile, gram negative, aerobic, cocobacilli, non-sporing and pleomorphic.
- Require X and V factors for growth. X factor is iron porphyrin haematin and V factor is a codehydrogenase. The former is necessary for synthesis of enzymes necessary for aerobic respiration and the latter functions as hydrogen acceptor.
- In blood agar colonies of *H. influenzae* are large with satellitism. Other media used are chocolate agar, Filde's agar, Leventhal's medium etc.
- Capsulated strains produce indole, reduce nitrate but fermentation is less dependable.
- Best preserved in chocolate agar slopes or lyophilization.
- Capsulated strains possess polysaccharide antigen based on which 6 types are identified; type 'b' strain accounts for most human infection.
- Pathogenicity ranges from meningits to epiglottitis. otitis, pneumonia, arthritis, endocarditis etc.
- Diagnosis is based on culture of organism from CSF, sputum, throat swab. Penicillin may be in-

corporated into the medium to prevent growth of other organisms.

- *Haemophilus aegypticus* causes conjunctivitis; *Haemophilus ducreyi* causes chancroid or soft sore; *Haemophilus haemolyticus* is a commensal of upper respiratory tract; *Haemophilus vaginalis (Gardenerella vaginalis)* causes vaginitis and cervicitis and *Haemophilus aphrophilus* may cause bacterial endocarditis and brain abscess.

*Haemophilus vaginalis* now called *Gardnerella vaginalis* is a Gram negative bacillus of normal vaginal flora. It causes vaginitis with malodorous discharge. In wet-smear one can see vaginal epithelial cells covered with many rods (*Clue cells*). The vaginal discharge is grayish, frothy with pH above 4.6.

There are many nontypable *H. influenzae* causing childhood otitis media, puerperal sepsis, sinusitis and pneumonia. Detection of polyribitol ribose phosphate, a part of capsular polysaccharide, immunoelectrophoresis, LA and ELISA can diagnose the infection.

*Moraxella catarrhalis* appear as gram negative cocci, some times occuring in pairs and retaining the side by side kidney bean configuration. They cause rhino sinusitis, purulent tracheo bronchitis and pnuemonia, *M. lacunate* causes keratoconjunctivitis. Other moraxella discovered from urine, blood, CSF include *M. urethralis, M. atlantae* etc.

## BRUCELLA

- Brucella are small Gram negative non motile cocobacilli arranged singly or in chains, nonsporing and encapsulated. Strict arobes with optimum growth at pH 6.6-7.4 at 37°C. Growth is slow and seanty. Addition of 10% $Co_2$ improves growth for *B. abortus* and *B. melitensis*.

- In nutrient agar colonies are small, moist, translucent and glistening with butyrous consistency. After 7 days incubation in MacConkey medium very small convex amorphous and yellowish colonies appear.
- They are catalase, oxidase and urease positive, reduce nitrates to nitrites but do not ferment carbohydrates.
- Basic fuchsin and thionine are used for differentiation. *B. abortus* and *B. melitensis* grow in presence of basic fuchsin and *B. suis* grows in presence of thionine
- Can survive in soil and manure for many days but easily killed by pasteurization of milk and 1% phenol
- Somatic antigen has two components A and M. In *B abortus* A is 20 times more as M, but reverse is for *B melitensis*. *B. suis* has intermediate antigenic pattern. Antigenic cross reaction occurs with vibrios. Superficial L antigen is present resembling the Vi antigen of salmonella.
- Tb phage lyses *B. abortus*; hence helpful in identification and classification
- All the three specics are pathogenic to man, *B. melitensis* being most pathogenic, and *B suis* being least pathogenic.
- Brucellosis can be acute, subacute or chronic. Acute brucellosis is called undulent fever. Blood culture rarely positive in chronic and less commonly in subacute brucellosis.
- Diagnosis is based on blood culture in trypticase soy broth, tryptose broth, thionine tryptose agar or liver infusion broth at 37°C with 5-10% $CO_2$. Subinnoculations are made on solid media every

3-5 days till 4-8 weeks. Castenda's blood culture bottle are preferred as the bottle contains solid as well as liquid media, minimising risk of infection to laboratory workers. Culture may be obtained from CSF, lymphnode, bone marrow, abscess etc.

- Agglutination test is more reliable, is positive 1 week after infection. Titre more than 1:100 indicates positive result. Prior cholera vaccination leads to positive agglutinin titre to brucella.
- Prozone phenomenon is common in brucellosis where agglutination test is negative in low dilution but positive in higher dilutions. This is due to presence of IgA blocking antibodies.
- Radioimmuno assay and ELISA can distinguish acute from chronic brucellosis.
- Complement fixation detects brucella IgG antibodies; indirect haemagglutination and indirect immunofluorescence are also sensitive and specific.
- Burn test or brucellin skin test is nonspecific that gives induration at test site in chronic brucellosis
- Other tests for quick diagnosis are rapid plate agglutination, Rose Bengal Card test, milk ring test and whey agglutination test.

## BACILLUS

- This group includes *Bacillus anthracis*, *Bacillus subtilis* and *Bacillus cereus.*
- They are aerobic, nonmotile Gram positive rods arranged singly or in short chains. The entire chain may be surrounded by a capsule made of D glutamic acid.
- In culture the bacilli are arranged end to end in chains (bamboo stick appearance)

- Growth on oxalated agar shows oval central spores
- Grow in nutrient agar with raised irregular dull opaque grayish white colonies; medusa head appearance under magnifying glass.
- Virulent capsulated strains form rough colonies and the avirulent forms—smooth colonies.
- In gelatin stab - characteristic inverted tree appearance.
- Selective medium is used to isolate anthrax from mixture of spore bearing bacilli. It consists of poly myxin, lysozyme, EDTA and thalous acetate added to heart infusion agar.
- Ferment glucose, sucrose and maltose with formation of acid but no gas. Reduce nitrate to nitrite; liquefy gelatin and are catalase positive.
- Spores can remain viable for years in dry state; can survive for week in 5% phenol but destroyed by 4% $KMNO_4$ or 2% formal dehyde.
- Contain 3 antigens - (a) capsular antigen in virulent strains (b) somatic polysaccharide antigen (c) somatic antigen. Only antibody to somatic antigen is protective.
- Virulent strains produce exotoxin that has predilection for reticuloendothelial system.
- Anthrax is primarily disease of cattle and sheep; human disease occurring due to contact and inhalation.
- Microscopic examination of exudate/sputum with gram stain or culture of specimen provide the diagnosis.
- Ascoli test is the precipitation test where infected tissue extract is brought in contact with anthrax antiserum leading to foramtion of zone of precipitation.

- The capsule can be demonstrated by Mc Fadyean reaction of staining with polychrome methylene blue.
- Immunoprophylaxis is with (a) alum precipitated or aluminium hydroxide adsorbed extraculture components of *B. anthracis* vaccine. (b) Stermspore vaccine.
- *Bacillus cereus* grows in food, produces enterotoxin causing food poisoning.
- *Bacillus subtilis* is nonencapsulated, does not produce any toxin except haemolysin. It may contaminate stored blood causing haemolysis.
- Aerobic spore bearers resembling *B. anthracis* are called anthracoids but they are motile, unencapsulated, grow in short chains, at high temp (45°C) not susceptible to gammaphage

## YERSENIA PESTIS

- Short plump gram negative nonsporing, noncapsulated rods with rounded ends and convex sides. Pleomorphism is common. Show bipolar staining (safety pin appearance)
- Aerobe and facultative anaerobe, growing well at pH 7.4, temperature of 27°C.
- Broth shows flocculent growth occurring at bottom and along sides of the tube with little or no turbidity
- On nutrient agar colonies are small and transparent but in blood agar colonies are dark brown due to absorption of hemin pigment
- Coagulase, catalase, salicin positive
- Easily destroyed by drying, heat and chemical dysinfectants.

- Have 18 antigenic variants; have two types of antigens - envelop antigen and somatic antigen. Group S was the causative agent of 1994 Surat plague epidemic.
- Produce (a) endotoxin, a lipopoly saccharide (b) another toxin with propereties of both exo and endotoxin. Virulent strains produce bacteriocin
- Plague can be bubonic, pneumonic and septicemic. Bubonic plague is due to infected flea bite, pneumonic plague occurring due to inhaled aerosols from infected patient.
- Plague was introduced to India in 1031-1032 from central Asia following invasion of Sultan Mohammad. Plague has persisted in wild rodents and the vector flea Xenopsylla is difficult to irradicate.
- Diagnosis is based on Gram stain of exudate from lymphnode, sputum, throat swab or blood that show gram negative cocobacilli with bipolar staining. Culture and biochemical reactions are confirmatory.
- Rapid diagnosis can be by PCR, bacteriophage lysis, fluorescent antibody binding, and IHA using *Y pestis* $F_1$ antigen.
- *Yersenia enterocolitica* may cause terminal ileitis, mesenteric adenitis, and gastro enteritis.
- *Francisella tularensis* causing tularemia is small capsulated nonmotile Gram negative rod resembling mycoplasma.
- In man tularemia presents with lymphadenitis, or influenza like symptoms. Primarily it is a disease of rabits transmitted by ticks and fleas.
- Diagnosis is made by culture of organism, guineapig /mice inoculation, and agglutinating antibodies (> 1:160) and PCR

- Immunoprophylaxis with live vaccine is available.
- *Pasteurella multocida* is a gram negative coccobacillus implicated in catbite infections.
- *Yersenia Pseudotuberculosis* resembles plague bacillus and shows motolity only at 22°C. It has 6 serological groups and 9 serotypes. In humans it has a typhoid like illness.

***Bartonella Infections*** are caused by *B. bacilliformis, B. henselae. B.quintana* etc. The small gram negative bacilli. *B. bacilliformis* infects RBCs causing oroya fever. It is transmitted by sand fly. Verruga peruna are skin lesions, often pedunculated and nodular. Diagnosis is from blood culture. *B. henselae. B. quintana* cause bacillary angiomatosis characterized by angiogenesis and neutrophilic inflammatory response. Diagnosis is based on histology of lesion and staining of organism with Warthin, Starry silver stain. Definitive diagnosis is based on DNA sequence analysis of 16S ribosomal RNA gene.

*B. quintana* in known to cause culture negative endocarditis.

***Donovanosis*** is caused by *Clanatobacterium granulomatis,* an intracellular gram negative encapsulated pleomorphic rod causing granulomatous lesions of penis. Diagnosis is based on discovery of donovan bodies within large mononulear cells in smear from the lesion. Organism can be grown in HEp 2 cells or chicken embryonic yolk sac.

## MYCOBACTERIA

Mycobacteria are acid fast, aerobic, non motile nonsporing, nonencapsulated, slowly growing bacilli. They require enriched medium with egg albumin eg. Lowenstein Jensen medium.

## Classification of Mycobacteria

A. Tubercle bacilli
*M tuberculosis* (human)
*M bovis*
*M microti*
*M avium*
*M marinum*

B. Mycobacteria causing skin lesion eg. *M. ulcerans, M. balnei*

C. Saprophytic mycobacteria e.g., *M. butyricum, M. phlei, M. smegmatis, M. stercoris*

D. M. paratuberculosis (Johne's bacillus)

E. Atypical mycobacteria (Runyon) - Photochromogens, scotochromogens, nonphotochromogens and rapid growers.

F. Lepra bacilli - *Mycobacterium leprae* (human) and *M. leprae murium* (rat)

## MYCOBACTERIUM TUBERCULOSIS

### *General Characteristics*

- It is a straight or slightly curved Gram positive, aerobic rod, 1-4 μ long, arranged singly or in groups. It is nonsporing, noncapsulated and non motile. *M. bovis* is shorter, stouter and straight with uniform staining in comparision to *M. tuberculosis* which is beaded or barred in acid fast staining. Acid fastness is due to mycolic acid in cell wall. Non acid fast rods and granules from young cultures (Much's granules). are also known which can cause tuberculosis.
- Optimum temperature for growth is 37°C with pH of 6.4-7. Growth is acrobic but very slow (generation time 15 hours), the colonies appearing in

2-6 weeks. Addition of glycerol improves growth of human types. The enriched media is prepared by adding egg, glycerol, potatoes, meat, bone marrow, asparagine etc.

- In liquid media virulent strains form serpentine cords. Otherwise growth creeps up the side from bottom, forming surface pellicles extending along side the tube.
- Diffuse growth occurs in Dubo's medium that contains Tween-80.
- In solid media they form dry, rough, raised and irregular colonies that are creamy white at first, becoming yellowish or buff coloured later on. The colony of *M. bovis* is smooth, flat and white breaking up easily the growth being dysgonic, inhibited by glycrol and non niacin producing.
- Solid media used are Dorset egg. Lowenstein Jensen and Loeffler's serum slope. Lowenstein Jensen is most widely used that contains coagulated hen's egg. malachite green, glycerol, asparagine and salt solution Agar based media are less sensitive but permit early microscopic detection of colonies. Culture is more sensitive than staining but takes longer time. 5μg of selenite in agar shortens the growth period to 3-5 days.
- The bacilli are more resistant to drying and chemical disinfectants. Moist heat at 100°C kills them readily but 5% phenol takes 24 hours to kill them.
- *Niacin test* : Human tubercle bacilli form niacin when grown in egg medium. 10% cyanogen bromide and 40% aniline in 90% ethanol are added to culture. Yellow colour indicates positive *Niacin Test.*

- *Aryl Sulfatase Test* is positive in atypical mycobacteria. The mycobacteria are grown in media containing tripotassium phenolphthalein disulphate. Red colour develops on addition of alkali due to free phenolphthalein in a positive test.
- *Neutral Red* - The virulent strains bind to neutral red in alkaline buffer readily and firmly than bovine strains
- *Catalase Test* - $H_2O_2$ and 0.2%. catechol in equal volume are added to 5 ml of test culture. Effervesence indicates positive catalase test and browning of colonies indicates peroxidase activity. Atypical mycobacteria are strongly catalase positive. Catalase and peroxidase activity are lost once mycobacteria develop resistance to INH.
- *Nitrate Reduction* is positive in *M tuberculosis* but negative in *M bovis.*
- *Amidase Test* - Five amides are used. Blue colour indicates positive test. The ability to split amides is used to differentiate atypical mycobacteria.
- *Virulence* - The genes responsible for virulence are (a) KatG encoding for catalase that protects against oxidative stress (b) rpoV that initiates transcription of several genes and (c) erP gene encoding a protein required for bacterial replication. There in differing degrees of susceptibility to tuberculosis in different populations linked to NRMP-1 polymorphism cloned to chromosome 2q.

**Antigenic Structure** - Group specificity is due to polysaccharide antigen but type specificity is due to protein antigen. Tuberculin testing employs proteins antigen.

- These are 4 bacteriophage types - A, B, C and AB.
- Mycobacteria don't have any toxin but induce de-

layed hypersensitivity after ingestion by monocyte macrophage system with sensitization of T cells. The initial reaction is usually inflammatory. Re-infection produces excudative and fibrotic - cavitative lesions. Bacterial polysaccharide induces immediate hypersensitivity and lipid stimulates accumulation of macrophages. Phosphatids induce formation of tubercle consisting of epithelioid cells and giant cells.

- When inhaled bacilli lodge in alveoli, are phagocytosed and reach hilar nodes. *Primary Complex* is subpleural focus with enlarged draining hilar nodes. Primary complex is an asymptomatic lesion undergoing spontaneous resolution making individual hypersensitive to tubercle protein. When immunity status is compromised, mycobacteria can disseminate from lung to cause meningitis, osteo myelitis, miliary lesions in lungs. Reinfection produces exudative fibrocaseative lung lesions. The bacilli are present in sputum and can infect people around.

**Diagnosis**

- Diagnosis is based on detection of bacilli in sputum/CSF; typical tubercular granuloma (central caseating necrosis with surrounded epithelioid and giant cells) on biopsy specimen and culture of organism. In Ziehl-Neelsen technique acid fast bacilli are seen as pink rods against blue background. Sputum is positive for AFB if it contains 0.5-1 lakh bacilli per ml. The use of AFB microscopy on urine, on gastric lavage is limited by the presence of mycobacterial commensals thus causing false positive results.

- Fluorescent staining is quick and convenient. The smear is stained with auramine phenol or auramine rhodamine fluorescent stain. When examined under UV light the bacilli appear as bright rods against dark background.
- Positivity can be enhanced by concentration methods like Petrof's method (centrifugation, examination of sediment), homogenization by 6% $H_2SO_4$/3% HCl; floceulation method, Jungmann's method etc.
- Culture in L.J. medium gives positive growth in 4-8 weeks. The colonies are niacin positive and non-pigmented with compatible biochemical tests.
- Drug susceptibility test be made by using resazurin or by introduction of firefly gene for luciferase when the drug resistant mycobacteria emit light.
- Drug resistance can be tested by PCR for rpo B gene to detect resisrtance to rifampicin.
- Serological tests like IHA, SAFA and ELISA are unreliable.
- Detection of tubercular DNA by PCR, DNA probe are more reliable with sensitivity of 1-10 organisms and 1000 organisms in specimen respectively.
- BACTEC-460 system uses radioleveled palmitic acid which is used as substrate by growing mycobacteria with release of labeled $CO_2$ and result is available in 8-12 days.
- Ribosomal RNA based probes have lowest detection limit of 100 organisms.
- Strand displacement amplification (SDA), QB replicase based gene amplification, gene probe amplified *M. tuberculosis* direct test are available.

- Humoral immunity has no role. In cellular immunity the $T_4$ helper inducer cells contain the disease through release of cytokines. While predominant $TH_1$ response provides protective immunity through release of 1L-1, 1L-2, TNF $\alpha$ and IFN $\gamma$, a dominant $TH_2$ response causes tissue destruction and progressive disease through release of IL-3, IL-5, IL-4, IL-10, IL-13, GM-CSF.
- *Tuberculin Testing* identifies people to have been exposed to tubercle bacilli or not. Purified protein derivative (PPD) 5-10 units is used as intradermal injection and result is read after 72 hour. An induration in excess of 10 mm x 10 mm is taken as positive. The test becomes positive 4-6 weeks after infection or BCG vaccination. *False Negative* test occurs in immunocompromised, malnourished, aged, concomitant viral infections, immunosuppressive therapy. sarcoidosis, HIV etc. Atypical mycobacteria and *M. avium* can give *False Positive* results.
- BCG can act as diagnostic as well as therapeutic test. This is a bovine strain made avirulent by 239 subcultures. It is given intradermally on deltoid and confers immunity in 60-80% lasting for 10-15 years, particularly the haematogenous dissemination leading to meningitis is reduced significanthy. *Mycobacterium habana* has been indeatified as alternative to BCG so also *Mycobacteriun vaccae.*

  *M. tuberculosis* possesses various protein antigens present in cytoplasm and cell wall and some secreted. The latter being important in T cell response. Antigens with protective role are 85 B and ESAT -6.

**Atypical mycobacteria**

They grow faster and in simple media like nutrient agar, at 20-25°C. They are pigmented, catalase positive, aryl sulfatase positive and often longer or shorter than typical mycobacteria. They are usually resistant to most antituberculous drugs.

**Nontuberculous Mycobacteria (NTM)**

Nontuberculous Mycobacteria (NTM) are ubiquitous in environment, hence their isolation from a site that is not normally sterile does not constitute proof of disease. Their identification depends upon morphology, speed of growth, pigmentation of colonies and by molecular probes where a colour is produced on hydrilization of the probe to specific sequence of micobacterial ribosomes.

NTM cause disseminated disease in immunocompromised. Mycobacterium avium complex (MAC) consisting of *M. avium* and *M. intracellulare* are responsible for most cases. *M. genavense* accounts for 13% cases and the rest is accounted for by *M. xenopi*, *M. simiae*, *M. scrofulacum*, *M. malmoense* and *M. celatum*. In immunocompetent persons. NTM also cause pulmonary disease (MAC, *M. xenopi*, *M. interjectum*, *M. kansasasii)*, lymphadenitis *(M. scrofulaceum)*, skin granuloma *(M. marinum)*, buruli ulcer *(M. ulcerans)* and infection of joint and soft tissues *(M. fortuitum, M. cheinae, M szulgai)*

Photochromogens produce pigment (yellow), only on exposuse to light e.g. *M. kansasii* causing chronic pulmonary disease. Scotochromogens produce orange pigment even in dark. e.g. *M scrofulaceum* causing cervical adenitis. Non photochromogens don't produce any pigment e.g. *M. avium/*

*intracellulare*, *M. xenopi*. The rapid growers grow in 3-5 days and are saprophytic e.g. *M fortuitum* causing resistant pulmonany lesion and *M. chelonei* causing abscess.

- *M. ulcerans and M. marinum* cause skin ulcer and granuloma. In skin lesion the former occurs in abundance but scanty in latter. The former has a slow growth but later grows fast (1-2 weeks).

**Table 8.4 : Difference between typical and atypical mycobacterium**

| *Group* | *Growth time* | *Colonies* | *Morphology* | *Pigment* | *Catalase* | *Niacin* | *Neutral red* | *Cord test* |
|---|---|---|---|---|---|---|---|---|
| HUMAN | 6 to 9 weeks | Dry | Slender | None | Moderate | + | + | Tight |
| BOVINE | 3 to 6 weeks | Dry Smooth Dysgonic | Short and thick | None | Moderate | – | + | Tight |
| GROUP I | 3 to 6 weeks | Dry Eugonic | Larger Beaded | Yellow or light yellow | Violent | – | ± | Slight |
| GROUP II | 2 to 3 weeks | Moist Smooth Eugonic | Large Coarse Beaded | Yellow to orange in dark | Violent | – | – | None |
| GROUP III | 3 to 4 weeks | Dysgonic Doomed | Small Bipolar beads | None rarely light yellow | Moderate | – | – | None |
| GROUP IV | 3 to 4 days | Usually moist and spreading | Large Incompletely acid fast | White to all colors | Variable | – | – | None |

**Table 8.5 : Difference between M. ulcerans and M. marinum**

| *Characters* | *M. ulcerans* | *M. marinum* |
|---|---|---|
| Distribution | Tropics | Temperate zone |
| Clinical course | Chronic progressive ulcer | Self limited ulcer |
| Bacilli in ulcer | Abundant | Scanty |

| | | |
|---|---|---|
| Rate of growth | Slow, 4 to 8 weeks | Faster, 1 to 2 weeks |
| Growth at 25°C | – | + |
| Growth at 37°C | – | + |
| Culture film | Bacillus in cord | No cord formation |
| Pigment in light | – | + |
| Mouse pad lesion | Edema, and rarely ulcer | Marked inflammation and purulent ulcer |

## Mycobacterium leprae

- It is long slender 4-5μ straight or slightly curved bacillus occurring in bundles of parallel packets. It is weakly acid fast, (5% $H_2SO_4$ is used for decolourization). In smear living bacilli are uniformly stained but dead bacilli are irregular and fragmented.
- Culture not possible in bacteriological or enriched media but has been grown on mousefoot pad, and LJ medium, fetal spinal ganglion cell culture.
- Generation time is 20 days
- Portal of entry is through skin and nasal mucosa, incubation period is 5-8 years. The habitat of leprosy bacillus is Schwann cells encasing the axon. It can also multiply in smooth and striated muscles. Leprosy bacilli are found in sweat gland, hair follicles, arector pylorum, tunica media of arterioles, dartos muscle of scrotum and smooth muscles of iris. Nasal secretions and ear lobule have plenty of them and bacilli can be found in sweat, semen, sputum, sebum, tears and breast milk of lepromatous patients.
- Disease occur in two forms - lepromatous and tuberculoid . In lepromatous leprosy host resistance

is low, lepromin test is negative and leprabacilli are plenty in lesion. In tuberculoid leprosy host resistance is good, lepromin test is positive and bacteria in the lesion are scanty.

- In borderline leprosy lesions have characteristics of both tuberculoid and lepromatous leprosy and they can evolve in either way depending on host resistance. In indeterminate type the lesion is unstable, often healing spontaneously.
- The genome of *M. leprae* is only 3 million base pairs, two thirds that of *M. tuberculosis*. Lipoarabinomannan is a key component of cell membrane and the outer capsule has specific glycolipid (PGL-1) which can be detected by serologic test. *M. leprae* is unique in having dopa oxidase activity

**Ridley and Jopling classification**

| | TT | BT | BB | BL | LL |
|---|---|---|---|---|---|
| Lepromin test | + + | + | ± | – | – |
| CMI | + + + | + + | + | – | – |
| Bacterial load | ± | ± | + | + + | + + + |

- In tuberculoid laprosy the patch is small, asymmetrical with raised edges involving face, gluteal region and limbs; peripheral nerves like ulnar, peroneal, greater auricular are thick
- Lepromatous leprosy, besides skin, involves mucous membrane, lymph nodes, eyes and internal organs. Skin lesions are multiple, symmetrical and small.
- **Lepromin test** - 0.1 ml of antigen is injected intradermally. Early reaction (Fernade's) occurs on day 1-2 lasting for 3-5 days with erythema and indura-

tion. Late reaction (Mitsuda) occurs 3-4 weeks after and is expression of immunity. It may become positive in BCG vaccinated persons. It is done to (a) classify leprosy (b) to assess prognosis and response to treatment. Lepromin positive patients respond well to drugs and have good prognosis. Conversion to lepromin positivity during treatment indicates improvement.

- ***Laboratory Diagnosis*** is based on discovery of leprosy bacilli in bundles within lepra cells in scrapping from skin lesion, nasal smear or ear lobule. A sneeze from untreated patient of LL may contain $> 10^{10}$ lepra bacilli. Both IgA antibody to *M. leprae* and genes of *M. leprae* can be discovered by PCR of nasal mucosa.

  Tuberculoid tissues are rich in the mRNAS of TH1 family of cytokines with 2:1 predominance of $T_4$ over $T_8$ cells. In LL there is 2:1 ratio of $T_8$ over $T_4$ cells.
- Immunodingaostic tests for leporsy include, Dot ELISA, fluorescent leprosy antibody adsorption (FLA-ABS), passive haemagglutination and PGL-1 test. Among them FLA-ABS is the most sensitive. They are useful for epidemiological study, identification of individual at high risk, early detection of disease and its prognosis. IgM antibodies to PGL-1 are found in 95% of untreated patients of LL but only in 60% cases of TT.
- Rat leprosy bacillus *Mycobacterium leprae murium* may occasionally cause human leprosy. It is a gram positive acid fast curved bacillus, claimed to have grown on chorioallantois membrane of fertile hen's egg.

# SPIROCHAETES

- Spirochaetes are elongated, motile flexible bacteria twisted spirally along their long axis. The finefibrils between cell wall and cytoplasmic membrane impart motility, as they have no flagella. The motility can be flexion - extension; corkscrew like rotatory, movement, and translatory movements.
- Pathogenic spirochaetes belong to 3 genera - Borrelia, leptospira and treponema.

## Borrelia

- Borrelia are Gram negtive large (10-30 μ long) irregular, motile, spiral organisms, stained best with Giemsc and Leishman stains.
- Can be cultured in chorio allantois membrane of chick embryo and Noguchis medium (Ascitic fluid containing rabbit kidney.)
- Cause relapsing fever with splenomegaly, jaundice and often meningitis. Organism is present in blood during first attack of fever but not during subsequent recurrences.
- Giemsa stain of peripheral smear during fever shows the large loosely coiled spirochaetes. Phage contrast microscopy and buffy coat darkfield examination are more dependable.
- Animal innoculation is more definitive. 1-2 ml of patients' blood is inoculated into white mice intraperitoneally and within 2 days organism can be demonstrated in mice blood.
- Serological tests are unreliable; Wasserman's reaction is false positive.
- *Borrelia vincenti* is obligatory anaerobe, gram negative, a normal commensal of oral flora that causes

gingivostomatitis in malnourished (Vincents' angina).

- *Borrelia burgdoferri* cause Lyme disease (named after town of Lyme in Conneticut, USA) transmitted by ixodid tick. Initial lesion is erythema chronium migrans followed few weeks later by arthritis and neurological symptoms. Rising IgM antibody against organism correlate with disease activity.

### *Leptospira*

- Leptospira are activily motile delicate spirochaetes with closely wound spirals, and hooked ends. They don't take any stain readily, hence only best seen under darkground illumination.
- Over 160 serotypes and 18 serogroups are known
- *Leptospira ictero haemorrhagica* causes Weil's disease with jaundice, haemorrhage from mucous membrances, splenomegaly and nephritis; human infection occuring due to water and food contamination by rat urine.
- The organism is aerobic, microaerophilic and can be grown on chorioallantois membrane of chick embryo.
- Chlorination of water kills them.
- Diagnosis is based on visible organism in darkgrund microscopy of urine, CSF or blood, culture of organism in Bijou bottles and animal innoculation.
- Serological tests include complement fixation test, indirect fluorescent antibody test and agglutination test.

## *Treponema*

- Treponema are very fine, slender, spiral organisms with pointed or rounded ends. They are actively motile showing rotational, backward and forward and flexion movements.
- Stain rose red with Giemsa stain; morphology and motility can be seen under dark ground illumination.
- Have not been cultured in artificial media or tissue culture. Pathogenic strains may be maintained on rabbit testis.
- Easily killed by drying, cold or heat but can be preserved in liquid nitrogen for 10-15 years.
- Have polysaccharide antigen, protein antigen and nonspecific antigens.
- · *Treponema pallidum* produces syphilis, *Treponema pertenue* - yaws; *Treponeana caratium* - pinta and *Treponeua vincenti* - vincent's angina (gingivo stomatitis).
- *Syphilis* can be congenital or acquired. Acquired syphilis evolves through primary syphilis, secondary syphilis and tertiary syphilis. The spirochaete is amply present in the hard chancre of primary syphilis and in blood and mucous secretions of secondary syphilis patient. In tertiary syphilis spirochaetes are few and the cardiovascular - CNS involvement represent delayed hypersensitivity.
- Primary syphilis is diagnased only by darkground microscopy of specimen squeezed from hard chancre. In secondary syphilis mucous secretions or discharge from condyloma reveal the organism. *T. pallidum* is 6-15μ long and 0.2μ wide with 6-14

spirals. The cytoplasm is surrounded by trilaminar cytoplasmic membrane and then by a delicate peptidoglycan layer and finally by a lipid rich outer membrane. 6 endoflagella wind around the cell body in the space between inner cell wall and outer membrane.

- The disease is sexually transmitted with incubation period of 10-90 days.
- Antibodies develop 6-12 weeks after infection. The nonspecific antibodies are tested with VDRL, Kahn and Wassermann reactions. VDRL is most widely used. 0.05 ml of inactiviated serum is taken to which is added one drop of antigen on a special slide with 14 mm diameter ring. The slide is rotated at 120 revolutions per minute for 4 minutes and then studied under microscope. Presence of clumps indicate positive test. VDRL can be false positive in leprosy, malaria, relapsing fever, SLE, RA and hepatitis. CSF VDRL is done in secondary and tertiary syphilis.
- Rapid plasma reagin test can be done on serum (not CSF) and the result is visible to naked eye as the antigen contains carbon particles.
- Wassermann reaction is a complement fixation test using sheep erythrocytes, antisheep erythrocyte serum and guinea pig complement. Haemolysis indicates positive test.
- *Treponema pallidum* immobilization test is most specific and in treated as positive if more than 50% of treponema are immobilized by patient's serum.
- *Treponema pallidum* agglutination test (TPI) *Treponema pallidum Immunt Adherence* (IPIA) and fluorescent treponema antiboty (FTA) tests use killed treponema.

**Table 8.6 : Sensitivity of Serodiagnostic tests in Syphilis**

| *Test* | *Primary* | *Secondary* | *Latent* | *Tertiary* |
|---|---|---|---|---|
| VDRL | 78 | 100 | 95 | 71 |
| FTA-ABS | 84 | 100 | 100 | 96 |
| MHA-TP | 76 | 100 | 100 | 94 |

## Mycoplasma

- Mycoplasma are gram negative filtrable pleomorphic organisms varying in shape from spherical to branching filements. They lack a rigid cell wall and but are surrounded by 3 layered membrane.
- They require cholesterol or other sterol as growth factor.
- Facultative anaerobe, growing well in heart infusion broth with 2% agar enriched with 30% horse serum and yeast extract. The colonies have fried egg appearance, central opaque granular area of growth surrounded by flat translucent peripheral zone.
- They utilize glucose, are nonproteolytic
- CFT, IHA and IFT tests are employed for detection of antibodies.
- *Mycoplasma pneumonae* causes primary atypical pneumonia with severe symptoms but paucity of findings. Onset is slow with fever, cough with blood tinged sputum and X-ray shows lower lobe unilateral consolidation. Disease is self limited with recovery in 1-2 weeks.
- Laboratory diagnosis is by culture of throat swab or sputum in mycoplasmic medium containing glucose and phenol red. Growth may take 5-10 days to appear and is indicated by production of

acid, betahaemolysis and agglutination of guineapig erythrocytes.

- Due to polyclonal B cell activation a host of antibodies are formed giving less credence to serological tests, Cold agglutinins and agglutinin for MG streptococcus are usually present.
- Immurofluorescence, haemagglutination inhibition and metabolic growth inhibition tests are more dependable than IHA
- *Ureaplasma urealyticum* hydrolyzes urea. It may cause nongonococcal urethritis and Reiter's syndrome.
- L-forms bacteria also lack cell wall but can be differentiated from mycoplasma by the facts that they are not filtrable, resemble parent bacteria antigenically and biochemically, don't require sterols for growth, have same base ratio as parent bacteria and revert to parent bacteria in presence of of 25% agar.

## Actinomycetes

- They resemble bacteria since they are thin, possess cell wall containing muramic acid, have prokaryotic nucleus and also resemble fungus as they have mycelial network of branching filaments.
- Actinomycetes are gram positive, anaerobic or microaerophilic non motile, nonsporing noncapsulated filaments that break up into bacillary and coccoid form *A.Israeli* and *A Erikonii* cause human infection. They inhabit mouth, colon and vagina.
- Actinomycosis is a chronic granulomatous infection with suppuration and discharge of sulphur

granules through multiple sinuses. Actinomycosis can be cercivofacial, abdominal and thoracic.

- Diagnosis is based on microscopic examination of sulfur granules to demonstrate the gram positive filament surrounded by zone of swollen club shaped structure (Sun ray appearance). The granules may be cultured anaerobically on brain heart infusion agar and thioglycollate broth.
- Less common actinomyces involved in human diseases are *A.naeslundi*, *A. odontolyticus*, *A. viscosus*, *A. meyeri*, *Propionibacterium propionicum* etc. Most actinomycotic infections are polymicrobial.
- Actinomycosis has been called "Most misdiagnosed disease" as it rembles neoplasm.

## Nocardia

- Nocardia are aerobic, gram positive acidfast organisms appearing as branching filaments with tendency to fragment to form bacillary or coccoid form.
- *N. asteroides* and *N. brasiliensis* cause pulmonary infection, meningitis and brain abscess. *N. madurae* may cause mycetoma.
- Mycetoma is localised chronic granulomatous lesion of subcutancous and deeper tissues of foot presenting as tumor with multiple discharging sinuses. Actinomycotic mycetoma is white to yellow but fungal mycetoma is usually black.
- Nocardia may grow on ordinary media forming dry granular wrinkled pigment producing (red or yellow) colonies.

## Listeria Monocytogenes

- It is small, coccoid gram positive bacillus, usually occuring in chains.
- It is non motile at 37°C but shows slow tumbling motility when grown at 26°C.
- It grows on ordinary medium with temperature 4-42°C. Colonies produce betahaemolysis on blood agar.
- Ferments glucose and salicin with production of acid but no gas. Does not ferment mannitol.
- Most human infections are caused by serotype 16 & 46. Spectrum of listeria infection ranges from meningitis to abortion, still birth.
- *Erysipelothrix indiosa* resembles listeria but is non-motile and haemolysis on blood agar is minimal. It causes local lesion and often endocarditis.

## Lactobacilli

- They are gram positive, nonmotile rods showing bipolar bodies and barred staining like corynebacteria.
- Grow best at pH 5 or less and produce lactic acid.
- Form the bacterial flora of vagina (Doderlein bacillus) and are present in intestine (*Lactobacillus acidophilus*) synthesizing $B_{12}$ and vitK.

## Anaerobic gram negative bacilli

- They form normal flora of mouth, respiratory tract, intestine and vagina; produce fowl smelling pus.
- *Bacteroides fragilis* is the prominent member of this group isolated from blood, sputum, peritoneum, CSF, brain abscess, urogenital and wound infections.

- Lack the endotoxin of gram negative bacteria but their capsular polysaccharide acts as the virulence factor.
- Grow easily on heart-brain infusion agar in anaerobic condition with 10% $CO_2$.
- *Bacteroides melaninogenicus* produces black colonies and is isolated from lung and liver abscess, intestinal lesion.
- *Fusobacterium fusiformis* is isolated from blood, CSF, bone marrow.
- *Fusobacterium girani* is isolated from wound infection and peritoneal abscess. It has spinning type of motion.
- Laboratory diagnosis of anaerobic infection is based on colony morphology, Gram staining, pigment production, fluorescence with UV light, and biochemical properties.
- Gas liquid chromatography based volatile fatty acid profile study can identify the species.
- Rapid diagnosis can be made by PCR, RFLP.
- Fluorescence production in wood's lamp based on enzymatic hydrolysis of 4 methyl umbilliferone provide presumptive diagnosis of bacteroids.
- Hundreds of anaerobic species form normal human flora. 500 species are only seen in stool. In the oral cavity the ratio of anaerobic to aerobic bacteria in dental crevices is 1000 : 1. In the colon bacterial count is $10^{12}$ per gram of stool with ratio of anaerobes to aerobes of 1000:1. In the vaginal flora $10^{9}$ organisms exist per ml of secretions with ratio of anaerobes to acrobes of 10:1.
- Besides *B. fragilis*, the other members in this group are *B. vulgatus*, *B. distasonis*, *B. uniformis* etc. Other

members of bacteroides family are Fusobacterium, Prevotella, Porphyromonas. *Prevotella bivia* and *Prevotella disiens* are most frequent isolates from vagina.

## Rickettsiae

- Rickettsiae are minute organisms having properties in between bacteria and viruses. (a) they contain both DNA and RNA in a ratio of 1:3.5 (b) contain muramic acid in the cell wall (c) contain enzymes for metabolic function (d) do not multiply outside the cell (e) multiply in cytoplasm of cell except for those responsible for spotted fever group which also grow within nucleus (f) produce only endotoxin but no exotoxin.
- They are pleomorphic coccobacilli, non motile, noncapsulated, gram negative.
- Do not grow in cell free media except *R. quintana* which grows on blood agar. Grow well in yolksac of chick embryo or chorioallantois membrane. Sulfonamides favour their growth.
- Multiply in endothelial cells of small blood vessels causing vasculitis, principally of skin and many internal organs.
- Contain (a) specific soluble antigens present in the surface (b) species specific antigen on the body (c) alkali stable polysaccharide antigen sharing with that of proteus $OX_2$, $OX_{19}$ and $OX_k$.
- Epidemic typhus is by *R. prowazekii*, prevelent in J & K, man being the only natural vertebrate host and body louse being the vector.
- Endemic typhus is caused by *R.mooseri*, a disease of rat transmitted to humans by rat fleas. Man to

man transmission does not occur and it is prevalent in J & K.

- Spotted group of fevers are by *R. akari* which is mite borne; *R. australis*, *R. conori* which are tick borne. In ticks transovarian transmission occurs and organism propagates from one generation to other.Rocky mountain spotted fever (RMS) is the most serious form of spotted fever where lesions appear on skin, buccal mucosa, palms and soles resembling epidemic typhus.
- Scrub typhus is caused by *R. tsutsugamushi* transmitted by trombiculoid mite, the rodents being reservoirs.
- Trench fever is by *R. quintana* (5 day fever) transmitted by body louse. Organism grows poorly on yolk sac but can grow on blood agar.
- Q fever is caused by *R. burnetti* transmitted by ixodid ticks among animals. Human infection is due to inhalation of infected dust or milk. Endocarditis is the most common clinical menifestation.
- *Laboratory Diagnosis* is by innoculation of patient's blood in yolk sac of chick embryo or animal inoculation. (male guinca pig/mice). In Q fever, besides blood, sputum and urine can yield the organism. In RMS fever skin biopsy can reveal the organism by immunofluorescence.
- Serodiagnosis is by Weil Felix reaction where (a) $OX_{19}$ positivity indicates epidemic/endemic typhus, RMSF (b) $OX_2$ positivity in RMS fever and (c) $OX_k$ positivity - scrub typhus.
- Other, scrological tests often employed are agglutination of rickettisal suspension, IHA,

microimmunofluoresence, radio isotope precipitation etc.

- Immunoprophylaxis is by live vaccine (strain E) for epidemic typhus; using formalized antigens prepared from chick embryo - for epidemic typhus. Q fever and RMSF.

## Chlamydiae

Chamydiae derive their name from characteristic inclusion bodies they produce in the infected cell. They have cell wall like bacteria and rickettsiae, multiply by binary fission, contain both RNA and DNA, possess ribosomes but don't grow in cell free media. They belong to two groups - Group A causing trachoma, LGV and inclusion conjunctivitis and Group B causing psittacosis and ornithosis.

| | *Group A* | *Group B* |
|---|---|---|
| 1. | Contain glycogen, compact and rigid inclusions | No glycogen, vacuolated diffuse inclusion |
| 2. | Predominant host is man | Birds and animals |
| 3. | Sulfonomide sensitive | Sulfonamide resistant |
| 4. | Infection localized e.g. eye, genital tract | Infection generalized involving lungs, joints, CNS |

- Exist in 2 forms - (1) elementary bodies - the extracellular infectious particles (2) intracellular initial bodies that divide by binary fission to produce large number of elementary bodies.
- The inclusion bodies are basophilic and that of Group A can be stained with Lugols' iodine because of glycogen matrix they posses.
- Lack enzymes to produce independent energy, hence depend on host cell energy rich intermediates.

- Gram negative, susceptible to ether, phenol, formalin at low concentration
- Contain group polysaccharide antigens common to all members of chlamydiae and specific antigens detectable by gel diffusion or by immunofluorescence.
- *Lymphogranuloma venereum* (LGV), a sexually transmitted disease, causes small papulovesicular lesion on external genitalia followed by suppurative inguinal lymphadenitis (bubo) in male and pararectal and intrapelvic lymphedentitis in female. Smear of aspirate from bubo may show elementary bodies. Frei's test is positive (intradermal LGV antigen produces nodule at injection site in positive patients).
- Trachoma is chronic kerato conjunctivitis characterized by follicular hypertrophy, papillary hyperplasia, pannus formation and cicatrization. Microscopic examination of conjunctival scraping demonstrates characteristic inclusion bodies with giemsa stain. However fluorescent antibody method is more sensitive. The organism can be grown in egg yolk sac.
- Inclusion conjunctivitis is acute and destructive. The organism can be seen as inclusion in conjunctival epitheial cells.
- *Psittacosis* is contacted from birds with patchy infillration of lungs, meningoencephalitis, endocarditis, arthritis etc. Organism can be isolated from sputum, and blood and can be cultured in egg yolk sac. Complement fixing antibodies can be demonstrated.

## Legionella Pneumophila

- It is a gram negative, aerobic nonacid fast cocco-bacillus; a pleomorphic rod with single polar flagella.
- Can be cultured on Mueller Hinton chocolate agar medium, Freeley-Gorman agar or charcoal yeast extract agar enriched with ferric phosphate at pH 6.8-6.9. The colonies are cream coloured round or flat with entire edge producing brown soluble pigment.
- Intraperitoneal innoculation of guineapig can yield the organism. It is catalase and oxidase positive, hydrolyzes hippurate, produces betalactamase and emits yellow fluorescence under UV light.
- Gas liquid chromatography reveals it to be rich in branched chain fatty acids.
- Produce protease, phosphatase, lipase, DNAase, haemolysin, cytolysin.
- Have 10 sero types, produce exo and endotoxin
- Produce acute fibrino purulent bronchopneumonia.
- Organism can be demonstrated by direct antibody fluorescent antibody staining of formalin fixed lung aspirate, bronchial washing or sputum.

## HACEK Group of Organisms

- These organisms are fastidious, slow growing, gram negative bacteria who grow well in presence of carbon dioxide. Species belonging to this group include several *Hemophilus Species*, *Cardiobacterium*, *Eikenella corrodens*, *Kingella kingae* and *Actinobacillus actinemycetemcomitons.*

- Among Hemophilus species the most common are *H. parainfluenzae, H.aphrophilus, H. paraphrophilus.* They are known to cause subacute endocarditis but *H. parainfluenzae* in addition causes pneumonia, meningitis, brain and liver absccccess and septiceemia.
- *Eikenella corrodens*, is a fastidious facultative gram negative rod forming normal flora of mouth and nasopharynx. It is known to cause endocarditis, respiratory infections, meningitis, brain abscess, choriomeningitis etc.
- *Actinobacillus actinomycetemcomitans*, a commensal of mouth has been associated with destructive periodontal disease, soft tissue infections and endocarditis, brain absess, osteomyelitis.

## Other Gram Negative Bacteria

- *Achromobacter xylosoxidans* is a part of endogenous intestinal flora and infects immunocompromised causing pneumonia, endocarditis with very high mortality.
- *Agrobacterium rodiobacter* has been associated with IV catheter related infections in immunocompromised, prosthetic valve and joint infections, peritonitis, urinary tract infections.
- *Capnocytophage species* include *C. gingivalis, C. ochracea* and *C. sputigena*. They are gram negative coccobacilli, faenltative anaerobe requiring $CO_2$ for their growth. They inhabit oral cavity and vagina. They have been associated with sepsis in immuno compromised particularly those with acute leukemia. In immunocompetent they cause gingivo periodontitis.
- *Chromobacterium violaceum* is a slender slightly

curved gram negative rod, a facultative anaerobe is known to cause severe sepsis and metastatic abscess. Patients with defective neutrophil function are particularly vulnerable.

- *Cryseobacterium species* include *C. meningoseopticum* and *C.indologenes* which cause nosocomial infections with endocarditis, meningitis, pnuemonia and septicemia; particularly through contaminated fluids.
- *Plesiomonas shigelloides* is a motile gram negative rod causing diarrhoea. In immunocompromised it causes bacteremia, cellulitis, meningitis etc.
- *Aeromonas Species* cause bacteremia in neonates, myonecrosis in patients of trauma, burn and bacterial gastroenteritis. Prominent in this group are *A. hydrophila*, *A.caviae*, and *A. veronii.* Aeromonas an produce skin lesions resembling ecthyma gangrenous caused by pseudomonas. Nosocomial infections related to catheter with meningitis, peritonitis, pneumonia can ocur.
- Many other organisms like *weeksella species*, *flavillmonas* species, *sphingobacterium species*, *protomonas species* can cause human infections.

## Kingella Kingae

- It is oxidase positive, non motile. Gram negative aerobic bacillus; forming part of normal oral flora.
- May cause infections of bones, joints and tendons, gaining access due to mucosal damage during tooth brushing/oral trauma.
- *Cardiobacterium hominis* is a Gram negative pleomorphic facultative anaerobe forming part of normal flora of GI and respiratory tracts. It grows slowly on blood agar and may cause endocarditis with embolization, mycotic aneurysm and heart failure.

# 9

# Virology

- Viruse are filtrable ultramicroscopic particles containing either DNA or RNA.
- They reproduce inside living cell using cells machinary as they don't possess cellular organization nor have enzymes necessary for protein and nucleic acid synthesis
- They multiply by complex fashion but not by binary fission.
- The largest virus is pox virus (300 nm) and the smallest is foot and mouth disease virus (20 nm).
- Viruses have characteristic shape e.g.; rabies virus-bullet shaped; pox viruses-brick shaped; influenza and polio viruses-spheroidal and bacteriophages - head and tail like sperm.
- The central core of virus contains nucleic acid (either RNA or DNA) surrounded by a protein coat-the capsid.
- The capsid has subunits called capsomere. Capsomere may have helical arrangement, icosahedoal arrangement or complex arrangement.
- Viruses can be enveloped or nonenveloped. The envelop is derived from host cell membrane when virus is released by budding and is lipoprotein in nature. The protein subunits of the envelop are called peplomers. Peplomers can have triangular spike (i.e., haemagglutinin) or mushroom shaped (i.e., neuramini dase).

- Heat, UV light, X rays and Gamma rays inactivate the viruses. They can be preserved in deep freezer except polio virus.
- Dyes like acridine orange, neutral red and toluidine blue penetrate virus particles and unite with nucleic acid making them susceptible to inactivation by visible light.
- Magnesium salts stabilize some viruses, chlorine and iodine may destroy them but lysol and dettol are ineffective against them.
- Viruses depend upon synthetic machinary of host cell for replication as they don't have biosynthetic enzymes. The sequences of viral replication are - (1) adsorption of virus into host cell through cell surface receptor which may be a lipoprotein e.g; poliovirus; glycoprotein - e.g. influenza virus (2) uncoating or loss of outer layer or capsid (3) biosynthesis of viral nucleic acid and capsid protein. DNA viruses synthesize their components in host cell nucleus except for pox viruses which synthesize their components in cytoplasm. RNA viruses synthesize their components within cytoplasm except for orthomyxo virus and paramyxovirus. This synthesis proceeds via transcription of mRNA from viral nucleic acid and then translation of mRNA into viral proteins. In oncogenic RNA viruses the ssRNA is converted to RNA-DNA hybrid by viral enzyme reverse transcriptase from which ds DNA is synthesized (provirus) and is integrated to host cell genome. This provirus acts as a template for synthesis of progeny viral RNA. This integration of provirus into host genome may also lead to development of neoplasm. (4) assem-

bly of virus from synthesized nucleic acid and capsid proteins (5) release of virus from the cell with or without lysis of the cell.

Incomplete viruses result from abnormal replicative cycles. Some have high agglutinin titre but low infectivity (magnus phenomenon). Some times viral assembly is defective or the virus is genetically defective, thus incapable of producing infectious virion. *Virines* are made up of small amount of RNA complexed with protein of host cell origin. *Prions* are infectious proteins without any nucleic acid. They are virus like agents, only sensitive to proteases, producing neurodegenerative diseases. Prions exist normally as innocuous cellular proteins but can transform to infectious particles.

- When same host is infected by two or more different viruses there can be recombination of viral genomes leading to formation of new genome, reactivation of inactive virus, complementation and interference i.e. inhibition of growth of one virus.
- Viruses can be cultivated by animal innoculation, tissue culture and chick embryo injection. Chick embryo has the advantage in that it is clear and bacteriologically sterile and does not have immune system. The sites for cultivation are chorioallantois membrane for variola and herpes; allantois cavity for influenza and paramyxovirus; amniotic sac for influenza and mumps viruses and yolk sac for Japneese B encephalitis virus, clamydiae and rickettsiae. Chick embryo is used for production of yellow fever vaccine (ITD strain) and rabies vaccine (flury strain). However egg innoculation is

limited to few viruses, and slight contamination of innoculum can kill the chick embryo.

Tissue culture of human and animal cells are frequently used for virus cultivation. It can be organ culture, explant culture, or cell culure. There are 3 types of cell culture (a) primary cell culture eg - Rhesus monkey kidney cell culture (b) Diploid cell culture and (c) continuous cell line (cells mainly derived from cancer cells). Vaccine production is from (a) and (b) but (c) is only used for virus isolation. Hela (human carcinoma of cervix cell line), K B (human carcinoma of nasopharynx), $HEP_2$ of (human epithelioma of larynx cell line), McLoy (human synovial carcinoma cell line), Detroit-6 (Sternal marrow cell line) are examples of continuous cell line culture.

Detection of virus growth in cell cultures is from (1) cytopathogenetic effect e.g; syncitium formation by measles virus, cytoplasmic vacuolation (2) stoppage of acid production due to inhibition of cell metabolism (3) hemadsorption i.e. guineapig erythrocytes will adsorb on the surface of the cell in culture (4) cell transformation by oncogenic viruses (5) fluorescent antibody staining (6) hemagglutination of tissue culture fluid as in orthomyxo and paramyxo viruses.

*Inclusion bodies* are virus specific structures seen within cell during virus multiplication. They have distinct size, shape, location and staining properties. Shape can be round, oval. pyriform or irregular. They can be acidophilic or basophilic. Vaccinia infected cells have Guarnieri bodies, rabies virus infected cells–Negri bodies in cytoplasm, herpes and yellow fever virus infected cells–Cowdry type A bodies, adeno and poliovirus infected cells–Cowdry type B bodies in nucleus. Inclusion bodies are both intranuclear and intracytoplasmic in measles.

## Classification of viruses

1. Based on affinity for different organ systems
   (a) Skin lesions - chickenpox, measles virus
   (b) CNS - poliomyelitis, rabies virus
   (c) Respiratory tract - commoncold, influenza virus
   (d) Visceral lesions - hepatitis, yellow fever virus
2. Based on epidemiological criteria
   (a) Enteric viruses - adenovirus, picorna virus, reovirus, hepatitis virus
   (b) Respiratory viruses - orthomyxo/paramyxo viruses, reovirus, rhinovirus, corona virus, adeno virus.
   (c) Arthopod borne (Arbo) viruses, togavirus, rhabdo virus, Bunya virus
3. Based on nucleic acid they contain—RNA and DNA viruses.

- Most RNA viruses are single stranded (SS) except for Reo virus and most DNA viruses are double stranded (DS) except for parvo virus.
- Besides strands of nucleic acid based on symmetry of nucleocapsid, presence/absence of envelop and number capsomers viruses can be further subgrouped.
- Major groups of DNA viruses are pox virus, herpes virus, adeno virus, papova virus, parvo virus and major groups of RNA viruses are - paramyxo virus, orthomyxo virus, rhabdo virus, arena virus,

toga virus, filo and flavi virus, reovirus, picornavirus, corona virus and leukovirus including retroviruses.

- Viruses have from a few to 200 genes. The RNA strand can be sense (+) or anti sense (-). Sense strand RNA genome can be translated into protein directly.
- Medically important positive strand RNA viruses include calci viruses, flavi viruses, picorna viruses and toga viruses.
- Medically important negative strand RNA viruses include bunya viruses, filo viruses, paramyxo virus and rhabdo virus.
- A lipid envelop is present in pox and herpes viruses; rero viruses, corona, toga, flavi, filo, arena, reo and paramyxo viruses.
- Retro viruses, lenti viruses and hepatitis B virus are not purely DNA or RNA viruses.
- Pox viruses are the largest DNA viruses and are unique among these viruses in replicating and assembling in cytoplasm.
- Retroviruses and lenti viruses differ from all other viruses in that they reverse transcribe themselves by their reverse transcriptase into partially duplicated ds DNA and then integrate into host genome. In HBV replication the reverse transcriptase transcribes the viral RNA into incomplete ds DNA which is not integrated into host genome.
- Viral replication is more error prone and many virions are imperfect as they have incomplete or imperfect genome. Adenovirus packaging is notoriously inefficient. Viral nucleic acid replication is more error prone than cellular nucleic acid repli-

cation. RNA polymerases and reverse transcriptases are intrinsically more error prone than DNA polymerases.

- Viruses frequently have genes encoding proteins that are not directly involved in replication or packaging of viral nucleic acid in virion assembly, or in regulation of transcription of viral genes. These proteins (a) directly or indirectly alter cell growth (b) inhibit cellular DNA, RNA or protein synthesis so that viral mRNA can be efficiently transcribed or translated (c) promote cells survival by inhibiting apoptosis (d) down regulate host immune and inflammatory response.

**Table 9.1 : Chemical composition of viruses**

| *Family* | *Nucleic acid* | *Mol weight* | *Protein* | *Transcription* |
|---|---|---|---|---|
| **DNA** | | | | |
| Parvo | SS | 2 | 3 | – |
| Papova | DS | 3-5 | 6 | – |
| Adeno | DS | 20-25 | 9 | – |
| Herpes | DS | 100 | 12-27 | – |
| Pox | DS | 160 | 730 | + |
| **RNA** | | | | |
| Picorna | SS (+) | 2-3 | 4 | – |
| Toga | SS (+) | 4 | 3 | – |
| Bunya | SS (–) | 6 | 3 | + |
| Arena | SS (–) | 6 | – | – |
| Corona | SS (+) | 9 | 16 | + |
| Retro | SS (+) | 10-12 | 7-8 | + |
| Ortho | SS (–) | 5 | 7 | + |
| Paramyxo | SS (–) | 7 | 6 | + |
| Rhabdo | SS (–) | 4 | 7 | + |
| Reo | DS (+) | 15 | 7 | + |

- Pox virus is brick shaped, rhabo virus is bullet shaped and others are spherical in shape.
- Capsid symmetry is helical for most RNA viruses except calci, flavi, corona, toga and picorna viruses where it is icosahedral. Capsid symmetry is icosahedral for DNA viruses.
- Envelop is absent in parvo, papova, adeno group of DNA viruses; reo, calci and picorna group of RNA viruses
- Pox viruses have complex capsid symmetry.
- Persistent or latent infection occurs in HBV, HCV, rabies, measles, HIV, HTLV, HPV and herpes viruses. High mutation rate accounts for persistent infection in HCV. HIV depletes $CD_4$ T lymphocytes and its *Nef* protein down modulates MHC class I molecules rendering HIV infected cells partially resistant to $CD_8$ cytolysis. In HSV and HZV lateney is established in nonreplicating neural cells. Intermittent reactivation occurs in HSV and HPV.
- Persistent viral infection accounts for 20% of human malignancies; HBV and HCV - hepato cellular carcinoma; HPV - cervical cancer; EBV - anaplastic nasopharyngeal carcinoma, Burkitt's lymphoma, Kaposi's sarcoma;
- All human cells can synthesize IFN$\alpha$ or $\beta$ in response to viral infection. IFN-$\gamma$ is produced only by NK cells and immune T lymphocytes in response to 1L-12. IFNs produce antiviral effect at transcription level.

## Laboratory Diagnosis of viral infection

- Serology and viral isolation in tissue culture are the principal ones.

- Detection of virus specific antibodies by haemagglutination, hemadsorption, and indirect immunofluorescence, but they are time taking, hence ELISA is preferred.
- Western blots measure antibody to multiple viral proteins simultaneously.
- Direct antigen testing of virus infected cell with virus specific monoclonal antibodies.
- Viral nucleic acid amplification by polymerase chain reaction.
- Measurement of viral RNA/DNA in peripheral blood.
- Viral genotyping and phenotyping for identification of drug resistant viruses.

**Immunization for viral infections**

- Small pox and polio vaccines have erradicated these two diseases
- Rabies and measles have been contained
- Threat of influenza pandemic has been thwarted through immunization.
- HBV vaccination has reduced acute/chronic hepatitis and hepatocellular carcinoma.
- Mumps and rubella vaccination is widely available.
- Varicella and HAV vaccines are now available.
- HPV vaccine to prevent cervical cancer is on anvil.
- Production of transgenic plants (potato, banana) expressing protective vaccine antigens can provide immunity when ingested.
- DNA vaccine is on the pipeline where DNA plasmid containing gene sequence for immunogenic protein is injected or inhaled to be taken up by cells to produce immune response but carries the

potential risk of integration of viral oncogenes from the vector.

RNA vaccine on the contrary is less stable and needs multiple injections but does not intigrate into chromosome or cause insertional mutagenesis.

## Pox virus

- It is brick shaped measuring 800 × 200 × 100 nm, having a central biconcave DNA core. It is covered by an inner coat adhered to nucleoprotein and an outer irregular layer. On either side of nucleoide are oval lateral bodies.
- They are susceptible to UV light, formalin and oxidizing agents. In dry state the virus may remain infective at room temperature for one year. In moist state the virus can be destroyed at 60°C in 10 minutes.
- The mammalian pox viruses include variola, vaccinia, cowpox, rabbit pox, monkey pox; that of birds include - fowl pox, turkey pox; and miscellaneous ones causing contagious pustular dermatitis, milker nodule, bovine pustular stomatitis.
- Possess about 8 antigens that include (a) LS antigen (b) agglutinogen (c) nucleoprotein (d) hemagglutinin (e) protective antigen. LS antigen is responsible for flocculation, precipitation and complement fixation. Antibody to it is not protective. Protective antigen is isolated during early stage of virus replication and antibody so it is also not protctive.
- The virus is cultivated in chick embryo or tissue culture

- In smallpox (now exinct) virus can be isolated from throat, skin lesions and blood. Light microscopy may show the Guarnieri bodies. Viral antigens may be demonstrard by CF, HA, PIG and immunofluorescent stains.
- Vaccination with Elstree strain, $EM_{63}$ and Newyork stain provide lasting immunity. The last case of small pox was reported from Somalia in 1977 and since 1980 WHO has declared the world small pox free.
- *Molluscum Contagiosum* is a benign disease characterized by pearly flesh colored umbilicated skin lesions, 2-5 mm without any inflammation or necrosis. The disease is contacted from swimming pools and is propagated by skin and sexual contact. Diagnosis is based on demonstration of cytoplasmic eosinophilic inclusions. The disease is extensive in HIV patients, lesions appearing anywhere except palm and sole.

**Varicella-Zoster Virus (VZV)**

VZV is a member of the family Herpesviridae, sharing with other members structural characteristics like lipid envelope, surrounding a nucleocapsid with icosahedral symmetry, diameter of 180-200 nm and centrally located dsDNA.

- Transmission is by respiratory route, harbored at nasopharynx with multiplication causing viremia with vesicles involving epidermis and dermis. Biopsy shows ballooning of cell, multinucleated giant cells, and eonsinophilic intranuclear inclusions.
- Lesions have centrifugal evolution, lesions at various stages of evolution can be seen; often involve oral mucosa and vagina.

- Herpes zoster is the consequence of reactivation of latent VZV from dorsal root ganglia, causing unilateral vesicular erruption within a dermatome with severe pain.
- Chicken pox and HZV are serious in immuno compromised.
- Confirmation of diagnosis is by VZV isolation in cell culture; demostration of multinucleated giant cells in Tzanck smear, PCR of vesicular fluid for DNA, fluorescent antibody to membrane antigen (FAMA) and ELISA.
- Immune prophylaxis is with live attenuated varicella vaccine often combined with varicella-zoster immunoglobulin.

## Herpes simplex viruses

- HSV is a linear double stranded DNA virus encoding more than 75 gene products, packaged in icosahedral protein shell (capsid) composed of 162 capsomeres. Between the capsid and lipid bilayer of the envelop is the tegument.
- Viral replication has both nuclear and cytoplasmic phases but is highly regulated by α, β, γ genes.
- Viral replication in nucleus produces two types of inclusion bodies (a) basophilic Feulgen positive bodies containing viral DNA (b) eosinophilic inclusion body representing scar of viral infection.
- Latency is common with transcription of a limited number of viral proteins but with subsequent reactivation and invasion of mucosal cells at opportune time.
- Monoclonal antibodies specific for each viral glycoproteins confer protection but in experimental infections only.

- HSV contains a gene called UL-12 that can bind to TAP-1 and reduce the ability of HSV binding to HLA thereby reducing recognition of viral proteins by cytotoxic T cells.
- The over all sequence homology in HSV - I and HSV - II is 50% HSVI causes oral-facial herpes and HSV II–genital herpes. Both can cause proctitis, meningo encephalitis, visceral infection.
- Immunoprophylaxis is not available but use of condom prevent sexual transmission.

**Epstein - Barr virus**

- EBV consists of a linear dsDNA surrounded by icosahedral nucleocapsid and the glycoprotein envelop.
- EBV is transmitted by salivary secretions, the virus initially multiplying in salivary glands.
- EBV receptor CD21 is present on B cells and epithelial, cells hence B cell proliferation causes atypical lymphocytosis.
- More than 10% of lymphocytes are atypical i.e. they have abundant cytoplasm, vacuoles and indentation of cell membrane. $CD_8$ T cells predominate among atypical lymphocytes.
- Infectious mononucleosis caused by EBV presents with sorethroat, lymphadenopathy and fever.
- Laboratory diagnosis is by detection of heterophile antibody, an IgM that does not bind EBV protein; presence of antibodies IgM, IgG to viral capsid antigens; antibodies to early antigen.
- EBV is linked to oral hairy cell leukoplakia, chronic fatigue syndrome, Burkitt lymphoma, Hodgkin's disease (mixed cellularity type), anaplas-

tic nasopharyngeal carcinoma and CNS lymphomas in HIV patients.

- Immunoprophylaxis is not availabe at present.

**Cytomegalovirus (CMV)**

CMV has a dsDNA, a protein capsid and a lipoprotein envelop. It has icosahedral symmetry, replicates in cell nucleus and can cause either a lytic and productive or a latent infection.

- Viral replication is associated with production of large intranuclear inclusions and smaller cytoplasmic inclusions.
- In cell cultures it grows preferentially in fibroblasts.
- Requires prolonged and intimate contact for transmission; can be transmitted sexually, blood and bone marrow. Once infected the individual probably caries the virus for life.
- Cytomegalic cells are 2-4 times larger and contain 8-10 μ intranuclear inclusions, eccentrically placed with surrounding halo (owl's eye appearance). They are present in salivary glands, lungs, liver, intestine and CNS.
- CMV produces mononucleosis, but in immunocompromised it causes fatal gastroenteritis, neurologic disease and retinitis.
- Laboratory diagnosis is by detection of CMV antigen pp65 in peripheral blood leukocytes, CMV DNA in blood/CSF and increased antibody titre to CMV antigens.
- *Human Herpes virus* 6 causes roseola infantum (exanthem subitum) and febrile seizure in childhood, often focal encephalitis; pneumonitis and disseminated disease in immunocompromised.

- $HHV_8$ is present in Kaposi's sarcoma and multicentric lymphoma (Castleman's disease) and lymphoma of HIV cases.
- $HHV_7$ is not linked to any disease except pityriasis rosea.

**Parvovirus**

- Parvo virus $B_{19}$ is a human pathogen causing erythema infectiosum, arthropathy, transient aplastic crisis and possibly rheumatic disease.
- The virus is small (20-25 nm), icosahedral, non enveloped single stranded DNA virus with an outer capsid formed by two structural proteins.
- It does not grow in conventional cell culture lines, and animal model systems but does replicate in invitro human marrow, umbilical cord, fetal liver etc.
- Parvo virus $B_{19}$ can be detected in throat swab, sputum and serum in infected patients. IgM and IgG antibodies against $B_{19}$ can be measured.
- Fetal infection may be infered from hydrops fetalis, and presence of $B_{19}$ DNA in amniotic fluid or fetal blood associated with maternal IgM antibodies to $B_{19}$.
- No vaccine is available but immunoglobulin prophy laxis be considered for pregnant women and patients of immunodeficiency.

**Human Papilloma Virus (HPV)**

- They are nonenveloped, measure 50-60 nm in diameter, have icosahedral capsids composed of 72 capsomeres and contain circular ds DNA genome of 7900 base pairs. The genome has an early (E) region, a late (L) region and a noncoding upstream regulatory region.

- Product of early genes $E_6$ facilitates degradation of tumor suppressor $P_{53}$ protein and $E_7$ protein binds to retinoblastoma gene product : $L_1$ gene codes for major capsid protein; more than 80 types of HPV are known.
- They produce plantar warts, common and flat warts, epidermodysplasia verruciformis, condyloma acuminata, Bowen's disease, Bowenoid papulosis, laryngeal papilloma, conjunctival papiloma, focal epithelial hyperplasia of Heck, intraepithelial neoplasia and cervical carcinoma.
- Malignant potential is high with 41, 20, 38, 30, 39, 41, 31, 16, 18, 33, 35, 45, 51, 52, 56, 58, 66, 48.
- While 6 and 11 are associated with laryngeal pepilloma. 16, 18, 31, 33, 34, 35, 39, 45, 51, 52, 56, 58, 66 are associated with cervical cancer; plantar wart is due to type 1, 2 and 4.
- Respiratory papillomatosis in children can be life threatening with hoarseness, stridor and often respiratory distress.
- The replication of HPV begins with the infection of basal cell leading to acanthosis, parakeratosis, hyperkeratosis.
- Neutralizing antibodies can provide protection in animals but no vaccine is yet available.

## Rhinovirus

- They are small (15-30 nm) non enveloped containing single stranded RNA genome. They are acid labile, completely inactivated at $pH < 3$; grow preferentially at 33-34°C, the temperature of nasal passage.
- Have 100 serotypes, cause common cold, exacerbation of chronic bronchitis and asthma.

- Most serotypes attach through ICAM-1, causing edema of nasal mucosa, engorgement of turbinates brought about by release of 1L-1, 6, 8, bradykinin, histamine and prostaglandins.
- Vaccine for prophylaxis is not possible because of myriads of serotypes.

**Corona virus**

They are pleomorphic single stranded RNA viruses, 80-160 nm in diameter. There are club shaped projections around the envelope - hence name corona.

- They are fastidious and difficult to culture in vitro, some strains only growing in human tracheal organ culture.
- Cause common cold and often exacerbation of asthma and chronic bronehitis.

**Respiratory Syncytial Virus (RSV)**

- RSV is a member of paramyxovirus, named so, because its replication invitro leads to fusion of neighbouring cells into large multinucleated syncytia.
- Size is 150-300 nm, viral RNA is contained in a helical nucleocapsid surrounded by lipid envelope bearing two glycoproteins - G and F; the former helping in attachment and the later in fusion. Antigenic diversity is due to difference in G protein.
- Produce severe bronchiolitis and pneumonia in children and common cold in adults.
- Nasal IgA neutralizing antibody correlates closely with protection than serum antibody.

**Adeno viruses**

- Are complex DNA viruses of 70-80 nm having an

icosahedral shell with 20 equilateral triangular faces and 12 vertices.

- The capsid has hexon subunits with group specific and type specific antigens and penton subunits primarily containing group specific antigens.
- Produce acute upper respiratory infection in children but type 40 and 41 cause acute diarrhoea, and type 11, 21 - haemorrhagic cystitis, type 8, 19, 37 - epidemic keratoconjunctivitis; pnuemonia and disseminated disease in immunocompromised.
- Diagnosis is based on detection of virus by nucleic acid hybridization from conjunctiva, sputum, oropharynx or saliva, stool, urine etc. or antigen by ELISA.
- Vaccine against type 4 and 7 has been used orally to control upper respiratory illness in adults.

**Parainfluenza virus**

- 150-250 nm enveloped virus containing single stranded RNA genome. The envelop is studded with two glycoproteins - one having haemaglutinin and neuraminidase activity and other fusion activity.
- The nucleocapsid is helical and codes for 7-8 virus specific proteins.
- Type I, II cause epidemic but type III occurs in all seasons. Type I causes severe laryngotracheo bronchitis, type III - pneumonitis and bronchiolitis in infants.
- Laboratory diagnosis is from growth in tissue culture; viral antigen detection by ELISA, PCR but antibody detection by HA, CFA are less dependable.
- No effective vaccine is available.

## Influenza virus

- Member of orthomyxovirus; influenza A and B constitute one genus and influenza-C, the other; the differentiation is based on nucleoprotein and matrix protein antigens.
- Influenza A virus is further sub typed based on surface haemaglutinin and neuraminidase antigen.
- The virions are irregularly shaped spherical particles 80-120 nm with lipid envelop from which H and N glycoproteins project.
- Through haemaglutinin virus binds to cell receptors where as neuroaminidase degrades receptor and helps in virus release.
- The inner surface of lipid envelop contains M proteins that help in virus assembly.
- The genome of A and B has 8 single stranded RNA segment
- Antibody against haemaglutinin (HI) is protective, laboratory diagnosis is based on isolation of virus from throat swab, nasopharynx, sputum. Viral nucleaprotein or neuraminidase can be detected by PCR.
- Inactivated vaccine against A and B provide 50-80% protection but be given annually to maintain immunity.

## Rota virus

- It is a reo virus consisting of 100 nm tripple-shelled icosahedral capsid surrounding a genome composed of 11 segments of double stranded RNA.
- Group A strains account for majority of illness in humans.
- The virus has two surface proteins $VP_4$ an $VP_7$ both of which are involved in viral neutralization

- The capsid protein $VP_6$ induces protective immunity.
- Single most important cause of dehydrating diarrhoea in children
- Diagnosis is based on detection of rotavirus antigen in feces by ELISA, PCR and DNA probe.

**Norwalk agent**

- They are plus sense single stranded RNA, 27-32 nm, of calcivirus group causing diarrhoea in children and traveller's diarrhoea
- PCR and ELISA are diagnostic
- Sapporo like viruses have more typical calcivirus ultrastructure and cause diarrhoea.

**Enteroviruses**

- Entero viruses encompass 64 serotypes – 3 serotypes of polioviruses, 23 serotypes of coxsackie virus A, 6 serotypes of coxsackie virus B; 28 serotypes of echovirus.
- They have single stranded RNA genome surrounded by icosahedral capsid comprising 4 viral proteins but no lipid envelop. They are acid resistant.
- The receptor for echovirus 1 and 8 is VLA - 2 integrin; for echovirus 7 is CD 55 and for coxsackie B is CAR.
- Humoral and secretory immunity in GI tract is essential for control of enterovirus infection.
- Capsid protein VP-1 is the predominant target of neutralizing antibody; confering lifelong immunity.
- Enteroviruses cause aseptic meningitis, exanthem, hand-foot and mouth disease, herpangina, myo-

pericarditis, conjunctivitis, pleurodynia, paralysis, pneumonia and generalized disease of newborn with DIC, hepatitis, meningo-encephalitis.

- Polio has been controlled with 3 doses of inactivated/oral poliovaccine containing all 3 serotypes that induce IgA and IgG.
- Reoviruses are double stranded RNA linked to neonatal hepatitis and extrahepatic biliary atresia.

**Measles virus**

- It is a member of family paramyxovirus. The virions are pleomorphic spherical structures with diameter of 100-250 nm.
- The inner capsid is composed of a coiled helix of RNA and three proteins.
- The outer envelop consists of a matrix protein bearing two types of peplomers - one is conical haemagglutinin(H) and the other dumb bell shaped fusion protein (F).
- Infects respiratory epithelium and then spreads to blood infecting all types of white cells; both viremia and viruria develop
- Multinucleated giant cells with inclusion bodies in nucleus and cytoplasm (Warthin - Finkeldey cells) are seen in respiratory and lymphoid tissue.
- Immunoprophylaxis is by live attenuated measles vaccine given once at the age of 9-12 months, singly or along with mumps and rubella. Immune globulin 0.25 ml/kg (mxm - 15 ml) can be given as postexposure prophylaxis.

**Rubella**

- A togavirus of 60 nm diameter composed of an inner icosahedral capsid of RNA and protein that is surrounded by a lipid containing envelop. The structural proteins associated with rubella virus are $E_1$ and $E_2$ (transmembrane envelop glycoprotein) and C (The capsid protein that surrounds the viral RNA). Only one serotype is known.

- Like measles the rash of rubella is immunologically mediated, its onset coinciding with the development of specific antibodies. Viremia can be demonstrated 1 week before and 3 days after onset of rash.
- Rubella is less contagious than measles, spread by respiratory droplets.
- The rash is maculopapular but not confluent with posterior auricular, cervical and suboccipital lymphadenopathy. Petechial rash in soft palate (Forschheimer spots) may be seen.
- Laboratory diagnosis is by ELISA for IgG and IgM antibodies; virus isolation in cell culture from throat swab, urine etc.
- Immunoprophylaxis is by live attenuated rubella vaccine RA 27/3 given at 12-15 months with second dose at 4-12 years that give permanent immunity.

**Mumps virus**

- Mumps virus in a pleomorphic paramyxovirus, 100-600 nm in diameter. The core is of RNA surrounded by glycoprotein envelop containing hemaglutinin-neuraminidas (HN) and haemolysin cell fusion antigen (F) besides matrix envelop protein. The other components of envelop are nucleocapsid protein and an RNA polymerase protein.
- Replication of virus in epithelium of upper respiratory tract leads to viremia followed by infection of glandular tissue and CNS.

- Laboratory diagnosis is by isolation of virus in appropriate medium from specimens like saliva, throat and urine during first few days of illness. ELISA can detect rising mumps antibody titre.
- Immunoprophylaxis is by live attenuated mumps vaccine (Jeryl Lynn strain) given IM at 1 year and at 4-12 years.

**Rabies virus**

- Rabies virus is bullet shaped enveloped single stranded RNA virus of 70-80 nm diameter. The envelope glycoproteins are arranged in knoblike structures. The viral glycoproteins bind to acetyl choline receptors, contribute to neurovirulence of the virus, elicit neutralizing and haemaglutination inhibiting antibodies and stimulate cytotoxic T cell immunity.
- The nucleocapsid antigens induces complement fixing antibody as well as T helper cell reactivity. Antibodies to surface glycoproteins are protective. The antibodies to rabies virus used in diagnostic immune fluorescence assay are generally directed against nueleocapsid antigen.
- Initial viral replication occurs within striated muscle at the site of innoculation, the virus spreading to CNS via peripheral nerve axoplasm at a rate of 3 mm/hr.
- Rates of infection and mortality are highest from bites on face; intermediate for bites on hands and lowest on bites on legs.
- Diagnosis is based on discovery of eosinephilic cytoplasmic inclusions, the *Negri* bodies within neurons of brain.
- Negri body is of 10 nm, made up of a fine fibrillar matrix and rabies virus particles. *Negri* bodies are

absent is 20% of patients, hence their absence from brain tissue does not rule out rabies. *Negri* body are most abundant in ammon's horn, cerebral ccr-tex, brain stem and dorsal spinal ganglia.

- Immunoprophylaxis is by human diploid cell vaccine or purified chick embryo cell vaccine. The 5 doses of HDCV are on 0, 3, 7, 14 and 29 given on deltoid or anterior lateral thigh (not on glutei). Pre exposure prophylaxis is with HDCV on days 0, 7, 21. On reexposure, they need only 2 doses on days 0 and 3.

## ARTHROPOD AND RODENT BORNE VIRUSES

### Bunya viruses

- All these spherical viruses have three negative anti sense RNA segments maturing into 90-120 nm particles in the Golgi complex.
- Most are mosquitoborne, causing sandfly fever, Rift valley fever, Hanta virus pulmonary syndrome etc.

### Flavi viruses

- They are positive sense single stranded RNA viruses that form particles of 40-45 nm in endoplasmic reticulum, trasmitted by mosquitoes and ticks.
- They include yellow fever virus, 4 dengue viruses, encephalitis viruses and haemorrhagic fever viruses including Kyasanur forest disease and Japaneese encephalitis.

**Reo viruses**

- They are double stranded RNA viruses with multisegmented genome forming 80 nm unenveloped particles.

**Toga viruses**

- They have single positive strand RNA genome, are of 60-70 nm size.
- Cause eastern equine encephalilis and Chikungunya fever.

**Arena viruses**

- They are spherical 110-130 nm RNA particles, usually rodent borne.
- Cause Lassa fever, lymphocytic choriomeningitis, South American haemorrhagic fevers.

**Filo viruses**

- Marburg virus and Ebola virus belong to this group, usually contracted from monkeys.
- The virions are 790-970 nm long, can have elongated and contorted forms with a lipid envelope confering sensitivity to lipid solvents.
- Contain a single linear negative sense single stranded RNA arranged in a helical nucleocapsid.
- The glycoprotein envelope has high sugar content leading to low capacity to form nuetralizing antibodies.

*Laboratory diagnosis*

- Rising antibody titer to the virus detected by ELISA
- Reverse transcription PCR

- Patients of encephalitis usually don't have viral antigen in CSF.

## HEPATITIS VIRUSES

### *Hepatitis A*

- Hepatitis A virus is a nonenveloped 27 nm heat, acid and ether resistant icosahedral RNA virus of the picorna virus family.

  It contains 4 capsid polypeptides, $VP_1$-$VP_4$. The virus can be cultivated in vitro. All strains are immunologically indistinguishable.
- Diagnosis is from anti HAV IgM in early disease; Anti HAV IgG predominates during convalescence.

### *Hepatitis B*

- HBV is 42 nm double shelled virion (surface and core) DNA virus with 3200 base pair complex multiparticle structure.
- HBV DNA codes for 4 sets of viral products from 4 overlapping genes S.C.P. and X.
- Instead of DNA replication directly form DNA template they rely on reverse trancription (effected by DNA polymerase) of minus - strand DNA from a 'pregenomic' RNA intermediate.
- Three particulate forms of HBV are known to exist (a) 22 nm spherical or long filamentous form representing excess viral envelop protein (HBSAg) (b) 42 nm double shelled intact virion with HBsAg expressed on envelop protein, the product of S gene; (3) 27 nm nucleocapsid core containing HBcAg and HBeAg. HBcAg does not circulate.

- HBV have 8 subtypes and six genotypes (A–F); however clinical course and outcome are independent of subtype and genotype except for an increase in 'precore mutation in certain genotypes.
- The protein product of S gene is HBsAg (major protein); the product of S region plus pre $S_2$ region is middle protein and product of pre $S_2$ and pre $S_1$ and S region is large protein. Complete 42 nm virus are enriched in large protein. Antibodies to all these proteins appear in serum.
- Nucleocapsid proteins are coded by C gene and are HBcAg and HBeAg. The C gene has precore and core regions; HBeAg being product of precore region and is secreted into circulation. HBcAg is not secreted into circulation.
- HPeAg in serum correlates with infectivity. HBsAg carrier mothers who are HBeAg positive invariably transmit diease to offspring but those with anti HBe rarely infect their offspring.
- The largest P gene codes for DNA polymerase which has both DNA dependent DNA polymerase and RNA dependent reverse transcriptase activities. The X gene codes for a protein that helps in transcription of both viral and cellular genes. HBxAg is associated with severe chronic hepatitis and hepatocellular cancinoma.
- Circulating HBsAg precedes elevation of aminotransferases and remains so during icteric phase to usually clear within 1-2 months, but does not exceed beyond 6 months. After HBsAg disappears antibody to HBsAg appears. A gap of several weeks may separate the disappearance of HBsAg and appearance of HBsAb. During this

window period anti HBc may represent serologic evidence of hepatitis B. Isolated anti HBc h o w - ever does not necessarily indicate active viral replication. Hence anti HBs is protective

- HBeAg is a qualitative marker and HBV DNA a quantitative marker of HBV replication. HBeAg represents high levels of viral replication and circulating intact virions. Pre $S_1$ and pre $S_2$ proteins are also detectable during replicative phase.
- Presence of anti HBc indicates non replicative phase when only spherical and tubular forms of HBV, not intact virions circulate. They are the carriers. Non replicative HBV can convert to replicative form spontaneously with appearance of HBcAg, HBcAb IgM and HBV DNA in blood.
- Precore mutants are unable to secrete HBcAg, tend to have severe liver disease that progresses rapidly to cirrhosis and does not respond to antivirals.
- HBV/$\alpha$ mutants (escape mutant) resulting from active/passive immunization leads to loss of neutralizing activity of HBsAb.
- Since the virus also occurs in lymph node, bone marrow, spleen, pancreas and circulating lymphocytes, recurrence of HBV is noted after orthoptic liver transplantation

## Hepatitis D

- Is a defective circular minus single stranded RNA virus that coinfects and needs helper function of HBV for its replication and expression.
- It is of 35-37 nm with hybrid structure, its delta core is incapsidated by HBs Ag envelop with some variation in major, middle and large HBsAg component proteins.

- Delta antigen exists in two forms - a small 195 amino acid species, which plays a role in facilitating HDV RNA replication and a large 214 amino acid species which suppresses replication.
- HDV antigen is primarily expressed in hepatocytes. In chronic HDV infection anti HDV titre is high.

## Hepatitis C (HBC)

- HBC is a linear single stranded positive sense 9400 nucleotide RNA virus of flavi virus genus.
- Structural genes at 5' end include the nucleocapsid region (c) and envelop region ($E_1$ and $E_2$). The E2 and adjacent non-structural regions are hyper variable regions. $NS_2$ $NS_3$ and $NS_4$ code for protease and helicase and $NS_5$ region for RNA polymerase.
- HCV circulates in low titre, hence not visualized
- HCV has 6 distinct genotypes, each differing from another by sequence homology of 30%. Anti HCV is not protective. Anti C22/C33 coincides with elevation of ALT but HCV RNA can be detected by PCR 2 weeks after infection.

## Hepatitis E (HEV)

- HEV is a 32-34 nm non enveloped HAV like virus with 7600 nucleotide single stranded positive sense RNA genome. It has 3 genes, the largest coding for nonstructural proteins involved in viral replication and the middle sized gene encoding for nucleocapsid protein.
- Both IgM and IgG anti HEV appear during infection.

**Table 9.2 : Serology in hepatitis**

| HBsAg | IgM anti HAV | IgM anti HBc | Anti HCV | Interpretation |
|---|---|---|---|---|
| + | – | + | – | Acute HBV |
| + | – | – | – | Chroni HBV |
| + | + | – | – | Acute HAV on chronic HBV |
| + | + | + | – | Acute HAV & HBV |
| – | + | – | – | Acute HAV |
| – | + | + | – | Acute HAV & HBV |
| – | – | + | – | Acute HBV |
| – | – | – | + | Acute HCV |

**Table 9.3 : Serology in hepatitis B**

| HBsAg | Anti HBs | Anti HBc | HBeAg | Anti HBe | Interpretation |
|---|---|---|---|---|---|
| + | – | IgM | + | – | Acute HBV |
| + | – | IgG | + | – | Chronic HBV |
| + | – | IgG | – | + | HBV, low infectivity |
| – | – | IgM | +/– | +/– | Window period |
| – | – | IgG | – | +/– | Carrier/past infection |
| – | + | IgG | – | +/– | Recovery phase |
| – | + | – | – | – | Post vaccination |

## OTHER VIRUSES

- *Nipah virus* is transmitted from pigs and is highly fatal.
- *Lissa virus* causes rabies like disease.

- *SARC virus.* The virus causes severe acute respiratory syndrome. It is air borne and the virus genome is more akin to corona virus.
- *Avian Flu virus* It is an avian strain of influenza virus transmitted to humans from chickens. The strain is H5N1. It is feared that this strain may swap genes with human strain to create an entirely new virus which will be more dreadly.

## RETRO VIRUSES

- The designation retrovirus implies that the information in the form of RNA is transcribed into DNA in the host cell.
- Retroviruses contain an RNA dependent DNA polymerase (a reverse transcriptase) that directs synthesis of DNA form of viral genome after infection of host cell.

**Table 9.4 : Retroviruses**

| *Subfamily, Group* | *Example* | *Features* |
|---|---|---|
| 1. Oncogenic viruses | | |
| Avian leukosis | Rous sarcoma virus | Contains *Src* onco gene |
| Mammalian C type | Abelson leukemia virus | Contains *abl* gene |
| HTLV | HTLV-1 | T cell lymphoma. |
| 2. Lenti viruses | HIV I & HIV II | AIDS |
| 3. Foamy viruses | Human foamy virus | No known disease. |

- All retroviruses are similar in structure, genome organization and replication.
- They are of 70-130 nm in diameter, have a lipid

containing envelop surrounding an icosahedral capsid with a dense inner core. The core contains two identical copies of the single stranded RNA genome. The RNA molecules are 8-10 kb long and are complexed with reverse transcriptase and tRNA. Other viral proteins like integrase are also component of the virion particle.

- The RNA has features of mRNA but it is not translated but transcribed into DNA called provirus.
- In cytoplasm the reverse transcriptase synthesizes double stranded DNA version of RNA template; this provirus moves into nucleus and integrates into host cell genome. This proviral integration is permanent but occurs randomly. Only lenti viruses are able to infect nondividing cells. Once a host is infected, it is infected for life.
- Retroviral genomes include both coding and noncoding sequences.
- In general, noncoding sequences are important recognition signals for DNA or RNA synthesis or processing events.
- The long terminal repeats (LTR) contain sequences involved in expression of viral proteins, integration. The coding regions include the *gag* (group specific antigen, core protein), *pol* (RNA dependent DNA poly merase) and *env* (envelop) genes. The *gag* gene encodes for 3-5 capsid proteins; *pol* gene encodes for reverse transcriptase, integrase and protease and *env* gene encodes for envelop glycoproteins.
- HTLV have a region between *env* and 3' LTR that codes for Tax (p 40) and Rex (p27) proteins that induce the expression of host cell transcription factors and regulate expression of viral mRNA.

- HIV I & II contain a larger genome than other retroviruses. They contain an untranslated region between *pol* & *env* gene.
- Retroviruses can be either exogeneusly acquired by infection with a virion capable of replication or transmitted in germline as endogenous virus.
- In general, viruses that contain only the *gag*, *pol* and *env* genes either are not pathogenic or take long time to induce disease because the pathogenesis of neoplastic transformation relies on the chance integration of provirus at a spot in the genome that will result in expression of proto oncogene.
- HTLV I causes adult T cell lymphoma, tropical spastic paraparesis and uveitis syndrome while HTLV II causes hairy cell leukemia.
- HTLV-1 has gp46, p14, p15, p19, p24, p21, p95 where as HIV-1 has gp 120, p6, p10, p17, p24, p64, gp41, and p34. HIV-1 has integrase in addition that facilitates insertion of provirus into host genome. The protease enzyme encoded by both HTLV-1 and HIV-1 cleaves the polyproteins encoded by *gag*, *pol* and *env* genes into their functional components.

## Human Immunodeficiency virus (HIV)

- HIV is icosahedral RNA virus containing external spikes of gp 120 and transmembrane gp-41. Gp120 binds to $CD_4$ molecules on T cell surface aided by coreceptors CCR-5 and CXCR4.
- The *gag* gene encodes for p24, *pol* encodes for reverse transcriptase, integrase, and *env* codes for envelop glycoproteins.
- The six other genes common to HIV-1 are *tat*, *rev*,

*nef*, *vif*, *vpr* and *vpu* which code for proteins involved in the regulation of gene expression. While *tat, nef*, *vpu* down regulate MHC class I expression thus evading $CD_8$ cytolytic T cells, *Nef* also down regulates surface expression of $CD_4$. *Tat* is immunosuppressive by inducing IFNγ from monocyte-macrophages.

- HIV 2 lacks *vpu* gene and contains *vpx* gene not contained in HIV-1.
- Molecular heterogenity in HIV-1 approaches 50% particularly in coding sequence for envelop proteins. One such region called $V_3$ is the target for neutralizing antibodies and contains recognition sites for T cell response.
- There are three groups of HIV-1; group M (major) which is responsible for most of the infections in the world; group O (outlier) and group N are rare. Group M has 8 subtypes (A, B, C, D, F, G, H and J) as well as 4 major circulating recombinant forms (CRFs) i.e. AE, AG, AB and AGI. While B subtype dominates in USA, subtype C is most common worldwide, E type is prevalent in India.

# 10

## *Mycology*

Fungi can be divided morphologically into 4 groups – moulds, yeasts, yeast like fungi and dimorphic fungi.

*Moulds* are filamentous and mycelial fungi. They grow as long filaments or hyphae which branch and interlace to form a meshwork or mycelium. The part of the mycelium that penetrates into the substrate absorbing nutrients for growth is called vegetative mycelium and the mycelium protruding to air is called aerial mycelium. On artificial medium they are seen as filamentous mold colony which may be dry and powdery. The pathogenic members are aspergillous, trichophyton, microsporum and epidermophyton. Reproduction is by formation of spores.

*Yeasts* are unicellular occuring as spherical or ellipsoidal cells. They reproduce by budding. On solid media they form moist compact creamy mucoid colonies resembling those of staphylococci. *Cryptococcus neoformans* is the only important pathogen.

*Yeast like fungi* grow partly as yeasts and partly as filamentous cells joined end to end forming a pseudomycelium. On solid media moist creamy coloured colonies are formed. The pathogenic member is *Candida albicans.*

*Dimorphic fungi* have two forms – spherical in tissues and mould like in culture media. The pathogenic members are histoplasma, sporotrichum, blastomyces and coccidiodes.

Based on sexual spore formation fungi are divided into 4 classes – phycomycetes, ascomycetes, basidiomycetes and imperfect fungi. Phycomycetes have nonseptate hyphae. They form endogenous asexual spore (sporangiospore) contained within sac like structure called sporangia. Sexual spores are also seen - oospore and zygospore. *Ascomycetes* form sexual spores (ascospores) within the sac, called ascus. They form septate hyphae and include both yeasts and filamentous fungi. *Basidiomycetes* reproduce sexually. Basidia are present on tip of the basidium. The basidia are sometimes leaf like structure as in musrooms. *Imperfect fungi* form a group whose sexual phases have not been identified. Pathologic fungus in this group is *Sporothrix schenkii.*

Many fungi can form two different types of spores and are given different names, depending upon spore bearing structures. When the spores are being produced by mitosis, the fungus in named anamorph (imperfect). Many fungi can have different sporulating structures in which genetic recombination occurs and are called teleomorphs (perfect). Most fungi that are pathogenic for humans are saprophytes in nature; they cause infection when airborne spores reach the lung or paranasal sinuses or when the hyphae or spores are innoculated into the skin. The fungi of ring worm, pityriasis versicolor and piedra infect the epidermis and its appendages; sporotrichosis and mycetoma usually arise from subcutaneous innoculations. Inhalation causes deep mycosis. *Candida albicans*, a normal commensal in mouth and intestine can reach deeper tissues when intestinal mucosa is disrupted. Aspergillous are opportunistic in that they infect hosts with compromised immunity.

*Pneumocystis carinii* is closer to fungi than to parasites by ribosomal sequences.

Clinically mycosis can be superficial, subcutaneous and systemic.

## SUPERFICIAL MYCOSIS

Dermatophytosis, tinea versicolor and candida cause superficial mycosis. Dermaphytes are fungi that infect skin, hair, nail and include trichophyton, epidermophyton and microsporum. *Trichophyton rubrum* causes tinea corporis/pedis/cruris/barbae/unguim. KOH prepartion of tissue/nail shows branching septate hyphae or chain of arthrospores. Culture on Sabouraud's dextrose agar at 25°C for 1-4 weeks shows velvety growth with red pigment on reverse side of the medium. Microscopic examination of growth shows long pencil shaped macroconidia which are rarely cigar shaped.

*Trichophyton mentagrophyte* in KOH preparation shows the spores surroundings the hair (ectothrix). Culture in Sabouraud's medium shows tan coloured cottony or powdery colonies. Microscopic examination of growth shows grape like clusters of microconidia.

*Trichophyton tonsurans* on direct microscopy of KOH preparation shows spores inside hairshaft (endothrix). In culture they form cream or yellow coloured colonies with central furrows. Microscopic examination of colonies shows the microconidia. *Epidermophyton floccosum* on KOH preporation shows smooth walled macrospores with 2-3 septa and have blunt smooth ends. In culture they form yellow to green colonies, wrinkled and folded with texture of suede leather. Microscopy from colony can show club shaped macrospores.

*Pityriasis versicolor* is due to *Malassezia furfur*. KOH preparation shows clusters of yeast like cells and short branched hyphae. It has not been cultured so far. Examination under wood's light gives yellow fluorescence. *Cladosporium mansonii* causes tinea nigra confined to palms causing dark brown to black irregular flat areas. KOH preparation shows brownish branched septate hyphae and budding cells. In culture colonies are moist shinny and black showing the budding cells and dark hyphae. *Piedra hortai* forms hard dark nodules on the shaft of infected scalp hair. KOH preparation shows dark brown dichotomous branched hyphae. Broken nodules show asci containing 2-8 ascospores. In culture colonies are greenish black, flat or elevated in the center. Microscopic examination from colonies shows dark thick walled hyphae, multiseptate with many chlamydospores. *Trichosporon cutaneum* causes white piedra involving the scalp or beard hair producing pale nodules on shaft of hair. KOH preparation shows on hair shaft transparent greenish brown mycelial mass. Hyphae are at right angles to shaft and segmented into oval cells but no asci. Culture shows rapidly growing shiny colonies which are first cream coloured. Microscopy of colonies shows transparent greenish brown mycelial mass which form round to rectangular cells.

## SUBCUTANEOUS MYCOSIS

*Rhinosporidium seberi* causes nasal polypoidal mass. KOH preparation shows fungal spherules containing endospores. Organism has not been cultured. Chronis blastomycosis is a chronic warty dermatitis of feet with warty ulcerating cauliflower like growth. KOH preparation shows dark brown round thickwalled fungal bodies with septae. In culture black coloured velvety growth occurs. The causative fungi are *Fonsecaea pedrosoi/compactum/dermatitides.*

Mycetoma can be madura mycotic (true fungi) or actinomycotic (higher bacteria). The fully developed mycetoma is a chronic suppurative granulomatous lesion with progressive destruction of contiguous structures. The granules are white to yellow in *Nocardia asteroides/brasiliensis* but brown to black in *Madurella mycetoni/grisea.* Under microscope actinomycotic mycetoma grains appear as very small gram positive bacteria like filaments but maduramycotic mycetoma grains have broad hyphae which are often septate with chlamydospore.

Actinomyces grow in Sabouraud's medium but for maduramycotic organisms Sabouraud's dextrose agar with chloramphenicol and cyclohexamide is used. *Sporotrichum schenckii* causes sporotrichosis which forms nontender red maculopapular granuloma at the site of innoculation and nodules along draining lymphatics. KOH preparation shows cigarshaped yeast cells. Culture on Sabouraud's dextrose agar shows creamy white and later brown to black colonies which are rough and yeast like. Microscopic examination of these colonies shows delicate branching septate hyphae. Pyriform shaped microconidia in clusters appear on lateral branches of these hyphae.

## SYSTEMIC MYCOSIS

### Cryptococcosis

Cryptococcosis is caused by *Cryptococcus neoformans* with involvement of brain, meninges, lungs, skin and bone. KOH preparation of CSF, involved tissue, sputum shows budding yeast cells and India ink preparation reveals capsulated yeast cells with budding. Culture on Sabouraud's dextrose agar shows smooth cream mucoid colonies. Microscopic examination from these colonies reveals encapsulated budding yeast cells. Precipitation, complement fixation, latex agglutination, counter current immunelectrophoresis can identify the cryptococcal antibodies.

## Histoplasmosis

Histoplasmosis is caused by *Histoplasma capsulatum* that involves lung parenchyma with hilar lymphadenopathy. Organism can be discovered from sputum, buffycoat of blood, urine, bone marrow, lymphnode and skin. KOH preparation, preferably Giemsa stained smear shows round to oval yeast cells present within the macrophages or free in tissues. On Sabouraud's dextrose agar with chloramphenicol and cyclohexamide there is slow raised growth, cottony at first, buffy brown coloured later. Microscopic examination from growth shows septate hyphae, delicate and branching, with smooth, round or pyriform microconidia and thick walled round tuberculate macroconidia. On glucose cysteine blood agar they form small mucoid cream coloured colonies which on microscopy show up as oval budding cells. Serological tests helpful in diagnosis of histoplasmosis are CF, LA, precipitation etc. Skin test with histoplasma antigen shows delayed hypersensitivity. The tissue lesions are characterized by granulomatous inflammation with epithelioid cells, giant cells and even caseation necrosis. Disseminated histoplasmosis coexists in patients who have tuberculosis, leukemia and Hodgkin's disease. An assay of histoplasma antigen in blood and urine is available. Nucleic acid hybridization can also be used to identify organism in culture. Despite the name, the organism is unencapsulated.

## Coccidiodomycosis

Coccidiodomycosis is caused by *Coccidiodes imitis*, causing pulmonary infection from inhalation of spores. The granulo matous lung inflammation usually heals up with calcification but blood borne dissemination may occur. The organism has two forms - growing as a white fluffy mould in culture media but as a non-budding spherule in host tissue. In Sabouraud's dextrose agar with chloramphenicol and cyclohexamide there is growth as white and moist thin cottony colonies. Later on they become matted and buffy coloured. Microscopically the growth shows up the septate hyphae that break up into endospores.

Direct microscopy of specimen from lesion or pus, sputum, urine, CSF shows the spherules, 30-60 μ in size with endospores. On blood agar without antibiotics, they grow as yeasts with similar microscopic appearance as above. Serodiagnosis is based on CF, precipitin, latex agglutination, and agar gel diffusion tests that detect the antibody to the fungus. Positive tests are least common among patients with solitary pulmonary cavity or primery pulmonay infection but always positive in disseminated disease. Skin test with spherulin is positive ( $\geq$ 5 mm induration at 24-48 hours).

**Blastomycosis**

Blastomycosis is caused by *Blastomyces dermatidis*, a dimorphic fungus that grows at room temperature as a white or tan mold but grows within the host or at 37°C as budding round yeast like cells. Infection is due to inhalation of the fungus from soil, decomposed vagetation. Patients have an indolent chronic course with consolidation, cavitation, fibrosis in chest X-ray. Mucous membrane lesions resemble squamous cell carcinoma. KOH preparation of sputum, pus, urine shows large (7-20 μ) spherical thick walled yeast cells. On Sabouraud's dextrose agar at 25°C they form white or brownish cottony growth, which on microscopy show septate hyphae with round or pyriform microconidia borne on lateral conidiophores. At 37°C incubation there appears wrinkled, waxy and soft colonies which on microscopy show thickwalled budding cells 8-45 μ in diameter. The fungus can be identified on the basis of its appearance, its dimorphism, the small spores borne on hyphae on mold form or from nucleic acid hybridization. Precipitation and complement foxation tests are also positive.

## Aspergillosis

Aspergillosis is caused by *Aspergillus fumigatus, A. niger, A. flavus* and several other species. Aspergillus is a mold with septate hyphae about 2-4 μ in diameter. Inhalation of spore causes self limited pneumonitis but in immunocompromised invasive aspergillosis can occur with multiorgan involvement. Aspergillus can colonize the damaged bronchial tree, pulmonary cyst/cavities forming aspergilloma which is non invasive. In patients of asthma aspergillus can aggravate the bronchospasm. KOH preparation of sputum or lung specimen show the septate filamentous hyphae. Culture on Sabouraud's dextrose agar with chloramphenicol at 25°C for 1-4 days shows green coloured colonies. Microscopic examination of these colonies shows septate hyphae bearing conidia in chain like fashion. Immunodiagnostic tests for diagnosis of aspergillosis is available by colorometric PCR and other PCR techniques. Mucormycosis is caused by *Rhizopus, Rhizomuor* etc. The organism in tissue is composed of broad, rarely septate hyphae of uneven diameter. Mucormycosis usually involves paranasal sinuses in debilitated diabetics or causes progressive severe pneumonia often with dissemination. The organism is difficult to grow from infected tissue but when growth takes place it is rapid and profuse.

## Candidiasis

Candidiasis is caused by *Candida albicans*. Candida are normal commensals of mouth, G1 tract and vagina. They can cause vaginal, esophageal and cutaneous candidiasis and often candidemia originating from IV catheters in immunosuppressed. Microscopy of KOH preparation shows yeast cells with budding and pseudohyphae which are Gram positive. Culture on Sabouraud's dextrose agar with chloramphenicol shows creamy white smooth colonies. Precipitation, agglutination and indirect fluorescent tests are positive in invasive candidiasis.

**Penicillosis**

Penicillosis is due to penicillium that causes otomycosis. KOH preparation shows small round spores and hyphae. On Sabouraud's medium they form colonies which are white at first but become bluegreen with velvity or powdery surface.

**Pneumocystosis**

Pneumocystosis is caused by *Pneumocystis carinii*, an opportunistic fungus invading the lung in immurosuppressed. In contrast to most fungi, *P. Carinii* lacks ergosterol. The organism has a small (1-4μ) trophic form; 5-8μ cyst form with thick cell wall containing up to 8 intracystic bodies. It contains two prominent antigen groups – (a) major surface glycoprotein (MSG) that facilitates attachment to host proteins (b) common antigen serving as a marker of infection. X-ray chest shows bilateral diffuse infiltrate biginning in perihilar region. Staining of sputum with methenamine silver, toluidine blue, cresyl violet selectively stain the cyst wall while Wright - Giemsa stain the nuclei of all developmental stages. Immunofluorescence with monoclonal antibodies is more sensitive than histologic staining. PCR diagnosis is also available. Bronchoalveolar lavage (BAL) specimens provide most dependable diagnosis. Transbronchial biopsy and open lung biopsy are reserved for patients negative on BAL. BAL provides organism burden, host inflammatory response and presence of other opportunistic infections.

# 11
## *Protozoal infections*

### Discovery of protozoa

| | | |
|---|---|---|
| 1836 | Trichomonas | Alfred Donne |
| 1843 | Trypanosome | Gruby |
| 1857 | Balantidium | Malmsten |
| 1859 | Giardia | Lambl |
| 1875 | Entamoeba | Losch |
| 1880 | Plasmodium | Laveran |
| 1882 | Sarcocystis | Lankester |
| 1888 | Babesia | Babes |
| 1903 | Leishmania | Leishman |
| 1907 | Cryptosporidium | Tyzzer |
| 1908 | Toxoplasma | Nicolle |
| 1912 | Pneumocystic | Delanoe |

Protozoa are unicellular organisms containing true membrane bound nucleus and cytoplasm. Protozoa have 4 classes (a) rhizopoda (eg. *E. histolytica*) (b) flagellates (eg. leishmania and trypanosoma) (c) sporozoa (eg. plasmodium and toxoplasma) (d) ciliates (*Balantidium coli*).

### Entamoeba histolytica

Three stages of parasite are (a) active trophozoites (b) inactive cysts and (c) intermediate precyst.

*Trophozoites* are 15-30μ, motile, with long finger like pseudopodia. The cytoplasm is divisible into clear translucent ectoplasm and granular endoplasm. Pseudopodial extension contains ectoplams into which flow endoplasm initiating motility of amoeba. Nucleus is 4 μ spherical placed eccentrically. It has well defined nuclear membrane with centrally placed karyosome. The *Precystic stage* is round or oval, 10-20 μ in size with sluggish pseudopodial activity. The cysts are encountered only in lumen of intestine. Cyst begins as an uninucleated body but divides by binary fission to form binucleated and quadrinucleated one. It is of 6-15 μ with clear and hyaline cytoplasm containing. oblong bars with rounded ends – the chromatid bars, 1-4 in number. A distinct glycogen mass is seen in early cysts. In quadrinucleated cysts chromadial bars and glycogen mass are absent.

The cysts are formed in human intestine and are passed in stool. Contaminated food/water with cyst when ingested, the cyst excysts in intestine and the metacyst containing the four nuclei is released. The nuclei divide by binary fission giving rise to 8 daughter trophozoites. The actively motile trophozoites pass into colon to cause flask shaped ulcers – the hall mark of amoebic colitis. The trophozoites can reach liver via portal circulation to cause hystolysis and amoebic liver abscess.

*Entamoeba Histolytica* can be divided into 22 zymodemes. Only 7 (II, VI, VII, IX, XII, XIII and XIV) are potentially pathogenic. Zymodemes refers to phenotypic isoenzyme patterns like glucose phosphoisomerase, phosphoglucomutase, hexokinase etc. Pathogenic strains also can be differentiated by DNA homology and base ratio, genome size and ability to grow at reduced temperature. Invasiveness also correlatee with phagocxtic process, collagenase, immunlogic cytotoxic proteins. Coexisting bacteria enhance pathogenicity.

*Diagnosis* is based on demonstration of trophozoites with parasitized RBCs or cysts in stool with cellular exudate and Charcot Leydon crystals. *E. histolytica* can be confused with *Entamoeba coli.*

**Table 11.1 : Differentiation between E.histolytica and E.coli**

| *Entamoeba histolytica* | *Entamoeba coli* |
|---|---|
| *Trophozoite* | |
| • 10-60 μ, single pseudopodium | 10-50 μ, multiple pseudopodia, |
| • Cytoplasm finely granular often containing RBC | Cytoplasm encloses bacterial debris as inclusion bodies |
| • Actively motile with invisible nucleus | Sluggishly motile with visible nucleus. |
| *Cyst* | |
| 5-20 μ, nucleus, 4 or less cigar like chromatoidal body, smaller central karyosome | 10-40 μ having upto 8 nuclei, a thread like chromatoid body, large eccentric karyosome. |

**Table : 11.2 : Differentiation between free living amoeba and *E histolytica***

| *Free living amoeba* | *E. histolytica* |
|---|---|
| Cell wall has pores | No pores |
| One nucleus | 1-4 nuclei |
| Contractile vacuoles present | Absent |
| Nucleolus large and distinct | Nucleolus small, indistinct |
| Mitochondria present | Absent |

*E. histolytica* can be cultured in Lock's egg albumin medium, Craig's medium, Balamuths' medium etc. Serodiagnosis by ELISA, indirect haemagglutination, latex agglutination are ony helpful in chronic disease. DNA probes are available for rapid diagnosis.

Non pathogenic amoeba commonly encountered are *Entamoeba coli*, *Entamoeba gingivalis*, *Endolimax nana* and *Iodameba butschii. E gingivalis* has no cystic form. The trophozoite is 5-35 μ, is actively motile. *E. nana* trophozoite has sluggish motion; its cyst has no glycogen mass, and its chromoidal bodies are spherical. *I. butschii* trophozoites are sluggish in motion; its cysts have large glycogen mass with one nucleus.

*Negleria fowleri* and *Acanthamoeba culbertsoni* are two free living amoebas that cause haemorrhagic acute meningo encephalitis (Negleria) or chronic granulomatous meningoencephalitis (Acanthamocba). *N. fowleri* exists in trophozorite and cystic forms. Trophozoites may be in amoeboid form or flagellated form (two flagella at anterior end). The cyst has smooth double cyst wall. Diagnosis depends upon detection of motile trophozoites in fresh CSF but serologic testing is not useful. Acanthamoeba trophozoites are larger than negleria, produce fine hyaline projections called acanthopodia and have no flagella. The cystic from has two cyst walls – the outer one wrinkled and polygonal but inner wall round. Nucleus is single, large and dense with centrally located nucleolus. Both organisms invade through nasal mucosa reaching CNS or cause fulminant corneal ulceration. Laboratory diagnosis is established by demonstration of amoeba, culture on nutrient agar with a suspension of *E. coli*/klebsiclla and serology (immunofluorescence and immunoperoxidase – in acanthamoeba only.)

**Table 11.3 : Differences between Naegleria and Acanthamoeba**

| | *Naegleria* | *Acanthamoeba* |
|---|---|---|
| Trophozoite | 10-30 μ one pseudopodium | 15-45 μ, many pseudopodia |
| Cyst | 7-10 μ | 9-27 μ |
| Culture | Positive | Negative |
| Tissue form | Trophozoite | Trophozoite and cyst |

## Giardia lamblia

*Giardia lamblia*, an intestinal parasite, inhabits duodenum and upper part of intestine. It has trophozoite and cyst forms. The trophozoite is 10-20 μ long resembling longitudinally cut pear. It is 6-15 μ wide, 1-3 μ thick, the dorsal surface being convex and ventral surface concave; the anterior end rounded and posterior end pointed. There are a pair of axostyle, two nuclei and 4 pairs of flagella. It multiplies by binary fission. The cyst is oval, containing 4 nuclei lying at one end or in pairs at opposite poles.

Giardiasis manifests with diarrhoea, malabsorption, flatulence and malnutrition. Diagnosis is based on demostration of cysts in stool or trophozoites in duodenal aspirate/intestinal biopsy. ELISA, indirect immunofluorescence and counter current immuno electrophoresis can detect the specific antibodies.

*Trichomonas vaginalis* is mainly found in vagina and male urethra. The trophozoite is 10-30 μ long, 5-10 μ wide, pearshaped having an undulating membrane coming upto middle of body, 4 anterior flagella, a prominent axostyle bifurcating the body, a parabasal body and anteriorly placed round nucleus. Multiplication is by binary fission along the longitudinal axis. It has no cystic form. Trichomoniasis is primarily a sexual disease causing frothy, fishyodor vaginal discharge and soreness. The trophozoite can be seen in vaginal discharge or urine (male) when stained with Giemsa, PAS, Leishman, acridine orange stains. It can be cultured in CPLM (Cysteine, peptone, liver, maltose) and Bushley's medium. IHA test employing trophozoite glycoprotein is also reliable. It can be confused with *Trichomones hominis* found is stool which has 5 flagella and its undulating membrane covers the full length. *Trichomonas lenax* a commensal of oral cavity is smaller (5-10 μ) in size.

**Leishmania donovani**

*Leishmania donovani* causes visceral leishmaniasis, an endemic disease of West Bengal, Assam, Western Orissa, Eastern UP, Bihar, and Tamilnadu. Man is the natural habitat, the organism being present in RE system of liver, spleen and bone marrow. It exists in two forms – amastigote (aflagellar) and mastigote (flagellar) or leptomonad form. The amastigote form is seen in cells of RE system. The promastigote form is seen in sandfly (the vector) and in cultures. It is pear shaped slender 5-10 μ long (15-20 μ in fully developed) with centrally placed nucleus; anteriorly placed parabasal body and blepharoplast. Undulating membrane is absent and a single flagellum exits from anterior end. The cosinophilic vacuole is the anterior most.

Culture in Novy, MacNeal and Nicole (NNN) medium, Schneider's medium, bacto agar biphasic medium with 20% calfserum grows the promastigote form. The amastigote form are round (2-4 μ) living intracellularly within PMN cells and monocyte. They have a large nucleus, the kinetoplast and the vacuole. The female sandfly, a small hairy fly feeding of fruit juice spreads leishmaniasis, usually biting at dusk or night. Visceral leishmaniasis (Kala-azar) produces irregular fever, huge splenomegaly, hepatomeglay, anaemia, pigmentation of skin and malnutrition.

*Laboratory Diagnosis* is based on demonstration of amastigotes (LD bodies) in blood, splenic/hepatic tissue/ bone marrow. Culture in aforementioned media grow the promastigotes in 7-15 days. Serum globulin level is very high which gives positive Aldehyde test (1 ml of patients' serum when mixed with 1 drop of 40% formalin gellification occurs). Leishmania skin test (Montegro test), a test of delayed hypersensitivity means induration of 5 mm of or more after 72 hour. of intradermal 0.1 ml antigen injection. ELISA, Indirect immunofluorescence, CFT be used to detect the antibodies. Monoclonal antibodies are also available for detection of leishmania antigen.

***L. tropica*** causes Delhi boil, a gramulomatous nodule at site of sandfly bite. The lesion may ulcerate and can have satellite lesions. The organism resembles *L. Donovani* morphologically and grows in NNN medium.

***L. brasiliensis*** causes granulomatous lesions of oral mucosa, nasal cavity and nasophanynx in central and South America. Trypanosomiasis endemic to Africa is caused by *Trypanosoma cruzi*, the parasite (amastisote) residing in RE system, CNS and striated muscles. transmitted to man by reduvid bugs. The disease can have acute form i.e. manifasting within 2 weeks of infection with fever and splenomegaly; a chronic form with psychic changes, spastic paralysis and autonomic degeneration. *Trypanosoma brucei* is a parasite of connective tissues, finally reaching the CNS. The vector is Tsetse fly that innoculates the infective metacyclic form.

Both the forms of trysenosomiasis can be diagnosed by demonstration of trypanosomes in peripheral blood, bone marrow, lymphnode aspirate, CSF. Culture can be done in NNN medium, serological diagnosis is by IIF, IHA, CFT etc. for detection of trypanosomal antibody.

## MALARIAL PARASITE

Malaria, a disease of tropics and subtropics (40°S to 60°N) is caused by *Plasmidium vivax*, *Plasmodium falciparum*, *Plasmodium malariae* and *Plasmodium ovale* (not existent in India). The parasite completes its life cycle in female anopheles mosquito and man. Female anopheles bite results in injection of sporozoites that settle down in hepatocytes and in 6-15 days come out of hepatocytes as merozoites. Some of these merozoites reenter hepatocytes where as others invade RBCs to complete erythrocytic schyzogony. In vivax and ovale preerythrocytic schizogony continues for years with intermittent liberation of merozoites and malarial relapse in absence of fresh infection. These dormant replicating parasites are called hypnozoites. In RBC the parasite assumes ring form, the trophozoite in which pigments appear. The trophozoites are transformed into schizonts. On maturity the schizont liberates thousands of merozoites to invade RBCs. The rupture of RBCs to liberate merozoites coincides with attack of malarial fever paroxysms. Some merozoites mature to gametocytes that enter the mosquito during bloodmeal. Micro and macrogametes are formed from gametocytes and they mate to form zygote or *ookinete* that penetrates stomach wall of mosquito and become an oocyst. The oocyst increases in size to 60 μ and contains the sickle shaped sporozoites. Oocyst containing sporozoites is called sporocyst. Sporocyst ruptures with liberation of sporozoites that migrate to salivary gland of the mosquito where from are injected to humans during mosquito bite.

The species of plasmodia differ greatly in their ability to multiply in the blood. *P. vivax* preferably invades the youngest RBCs, and the *P malariae* the oldest. *P. falciparum* parasitizes RBCs of all ages. *P. falciparum* multiplies more rapidly with high level of parasitemia, capillary plugging, increased vascular permeability and local tissue anoxia which contribute to renal failure, shock lung and cerebral malaria. Haemolysis of parasitized RBC causes jaundice and haemoglobinuria. Hepatosplenomagaly occurs due to reticulo endothelial hyperplasia. Anaemia develops rapidly. *Plasmidium falciparum* does not multiply in RBCs deficient in $G_6$PD or having HbS. Infants, are also protected because of HbF.

*Laboratory Diagnosis* of malaria is by examination of bloodslide taken at height of temperature. The thick smear is used for visualizing the malarial parasite and the thin smear for species identification. Examination of buffy coat is more definitive and can detect the parasite even at 10/cmm. Rapid diagnostic kits for falciparum and vivax malaria are available based on antibody to histidine rich protein (HRP-2) of developing parasite. PCR and DNA probes, monoclonal antibody based tests are rarely required.

**Table :11.4 : Morphological features in different species of malaria parasites**

| | *P. falciparum* | *P. vivax* | *P. malariae* | *P. ovale* |
|---|---|---|---|---|
| RBC | | | | |
| Size | Normal | Enlarged | Normal | Enlarged |
| Shape | Round and crenated | Round | Round | Oval or round |
| Color | Normal | Pale | Normal | Normal |
| Stippling | Maurer's | Schuffner's | Ziemann's | Jame's |

| | | | | |
|---|---|---|---|---|
| | dots (large red) | dots (Small red) | dots | dots (many small red) |
| Pigment | Black or dark brown | Fine golden brown in cytoplasm | Blak or brown | Black or brown |
| Parasite | Small, dark multiple infection of one RBC | Large, single | Tendency to form band across the RBC | Regular shape |
| Stages in PBF | Only rings and Gametocytes | Trophozoites Schizonts Gametocytes | Trophozoites Schizonts Gametocytes | Trophozoites Schizonts |
| Gametocytes | | | | |
| Ring Stage | Small, 1.5 μ, double chroma-tin, multiple rings | Large 2.5 μ single thicker chromatin | Characters of *P. vivax* | Characters of *P. vivax* |
| Trophozoites | Compact, small, no vacuole seen | Large irregular ameboid, vacuole, prominent thick chromatin | Band formation | Compact, chromatin is large irregular clumps |
| Schizont | Small Compact Not seen in PBF | Large, filling RBC Yellow brown pigment | Fills RBC Segmented, Daisy head pigment (dark brown) | Fill 3/4th RBC Segmented Dark yellow brown pigment |
| Micro-gemetocyte | Larger than RBC Kidney shaped Cytoplasm blue Fine granules scattered In smear many | Fills enlarged RBC Round Cytoplasm pale blue Many | Smaller than RBC Round Cytoplasm pale blue, Pigment | Of the size of RBC Round Cytoplasm pale blue Pigment and chro |

| | | | |
|---|---|---|---|
| in number | brown granules | & chromatin like *P. vivax* | matin as in *P. vivax* |

## TOXOPLASMA GONDII

*Toxoplasma gondii* causes toxoplasmosis, a disease contacted from cats. The protozoa has three forms oocysts,trophozoites and cysts. Trophozoites are oval or crescent shaped; lack flagella, cilia, and pseudopodia; have asexual multiplication. Tissue cysts contain thousands of organisms and transmit the disease. They predominantly involve skeletal muscles, heart muscle, and brain. Oocysts are present in cat feces and develop in soil and water to infective form –the sporozoites. The ingested sporozoites in man liberate merozoites that enter lymphatics and blood to develop into tissue cysts. Oocysts are only formed in cat intestine (not human) where merozoites transform to gametocytes and fertilize to form oocyst. Congenital toxoslasmosis can cause chorioretinitis, blindness, seizure, mental retardation, still birth due to tissue cysts. Patients with immunodeficincy, malignancy are especially vulnerable for toxoplasma infection.

***Laboratory diagnosis*** is dependent upon (1) demonstration of trophozoites or cysts in CSF, bone marrow, amniotic fluid, placenta (2) antibody detection by latex agglutination, IHA, ELISA, indirect immunoflurescense, (3) methylene blue test of Sabin and Feldman. High toxoplasma IgA/ IgM antibodies (>300 IU/ml) indicate recent toxoplasma infection.

***Isospora belli***, an intestinal protozoa causes mild diarrhea. Ingestion of oocyst in contaminated water releases 8 sporozoites in intestine which penetrate epithelium and give rise to trophozoites. Trophozoites undergo gametogony and form oocysts to be passed in faeces. Oocyst has two layered cell wall, oval in shape, has 2 sporoblasts/sporocysts.

***Cryptosporidiosis*** is caused by *Cryptosporidium seberi/* parvum whose oocyst is seen in stool (4-5 μ) that contains 1-6 large dark granules and many small granules. It can have thin or thick cyst wall. On ingestion of oocyst excystation occurs in small intestine with liberation of sporozoites which are transformed to merozoites and gametocytes.

Fertilization occurs with formation of oocyst, the life cycle being completed in one host. Diagnosis is based on discovery of oocyst in stool by concentration method/ Sheather's method. It takes red stain with modified acid fast stains. Serodiagnosis is based on ELISA and indirect immunofluorescence. Intractable diarrhoea in HIV patients is often due to cryptosporidiosis.

**Babesia** is a pear shaped plasmodia like protozoan transmitted to humans by ixodes ticks. Like malarial parasite, the RBCs are invaded with their destruction. Peripheral smear can show the ring shaped and amoeboid shaped parasites stained with Giemsa or wright stain. The disease is not seen in India.

**Balantidium coli** is the largest protozoal parasite inhabiting human intestine.

The trophozoites are oval 50-200 μ × 40-70 μ, the surface studded with cilia. The cytoplasm contains kidney shaped large macronucleus and small micronucleus. The cysts are oval with double layered wall. No intermediate host is required.

# 12

# *Helminthology*

**Discovery of Helminths**

| | | |
|---|---|---|
| 1685 | Echinococcus | Hastman |
| 1758 | Ascasis Fasciola | Linnaeus |
| 1782 | Taenia | Goezy |
| 1821 | Trichinella | Tidemann |
| 1851 | Schistosoma | Bilharz |
| 1853 | Dracunculus | Bastion |
| 1863 | Wuchereria | Demarquay |
| 1875 | Chlonorchis | Mc Connel |
| 1876 | Strongyloides | Normand |
| 1878 | Paragonimus | Kerbert |
| 1911 | Ancylostoma | Looss |
| 1952 | Toxocara | Beaver |
| 1960 | Anisakis | Van Thiel |
| 1964 | Angiostrongylus | Beaver |

**Trichinella spiralis** is a parasite buried in duodenal/ jejunal mucosa. Infection is acquired by easting viable encysted larvae in raw or uncooked pork. The larvae rapidly mature and mate, and the adult female then burrows into the mucosa of small intestine. Within 4-5 days the female begins to discharge viviparous larvae that are diseminated via the lymphatics and blood stream to most body tissues, usually oocysting in striated muscles. In intestinal phase there is diarrhoea and cramp and in muscle invasion phase - muscle pain and tenderness, periorbital.facial edema. Diagnosis is based on discovery of adult worm in feces, larvae in blood/duodenal washing/involved skeletal muscle biopsy. Circulating antigens can be discovered 2 weeks after infection. Bentonite flocculation test (positive titre ≥ 1:5) is highly sensitive and 100% specific. IgM and IgG ELISA are also dependable.

*Trichuriasis* is caused by *Trichuris trichura*, an infection most frequent in children. The slender worm is 30-50mm long attaching to intestinal mucosa by anterior whip like end. Eggs are passed in feces which mature to infective larva in the soil. The ingested larva hatch in small intestine and mature in large bowel. The diagnosis is established by discovery of barrel shaped eggs, in stool, 25-50 μ, the outer shell bile stained, enclosing unsegmented embryo.

*Ascariasis* is caused by *Ascaris lumbricoides*, the adultworm living in upper small intestinc. After fertilization the female produces large number of eggs that pass in the feces. The freshly passed fertilized eggs contain unsegmented ovum which becomes infective after 9-15 days, once rhabditiform larvae develop within. Once swallowed the larva come out in intestine, penetrate the intestinal mucosa, & reaches portal circulation, the lungs, ascend up the bronchi to reach pharynx and descend down the esophagus to reach intestine. They moult 4 times enroute and develop into adult worms (male and female).

*Diagnosis* is based on discovery of adult worm or eggs in stool. Adult worm is elongated cylindrical measuring 15-50 cm, male worm being smaller than female. The fertilized egg is 45-75 μ × 35-50 μ with three layers, the outer most being laminated. It contains the unsegmented embryo and floats in saturated salt solutions. Unfertilized egg. is larger, embryo is disorganized containing refractile granules. It lacks inner most vitelline layer and does not float in saturated salt solution.

***Ankylostomiasis*** is caused by *Ankylostoma duodenale* and *Necator americanus*. The adult worm lives in jejunum attached to the mucosa and lays eggs that are passed in stool, containing segmented embryo. In soil rhabiditiform larva is liberated which moults twice and becomes filariform larva which is infective. This filariform larva penetrates the intact skin; through lymphatics and venous blood reaches lungs, ascends up the bornchi to reach jejunum where it develops to adult worm, moulting 4 times enroute.

*Diagnosis* is based on discovery of eggs in stoool. The adult worm is pinkish 11-13 mm long, fusiform in shape with curved anterior end. The oral cavity has single pair of dorsal teeth and 2 pairs of ventral teeth. The ovum measures 75 μ × 40 μ containing segmented ovum (4 segments). There is a clear space between egg shell and segmented ovum. It floats in saturated saline and is non bilestained. Adult worm of *Necator americanus* is smaller, more slender having 4 teeth in buccal capsule.

Continuous sucking of blood by adult worms causes anaemia.

***Strongyloidiasis*** is caused by *Strongyloid stercoralis*. The adult worm lives in mucous membrane of small intestine. The eggs 30 μ × 5 μ are oval, transparent and hatch in intestine to liberate rhabditiform larva that are passed in stool. They penetrate intact skin and reach intestine of new host like ankylostoma larva and mature to adult worm.

The diagnosis is based on detection of rhabditiform larva in freshly passed stool.

***Enterobiosis*** is caused by *Enterobius vermicularis* (thread worm). The adult worms, 5-10 mm - live in intestine. Male dies after fertilization and the gravid female passes down to lay eggs around anus. The eggs are colourless, planoconvex 60 μ × 30 μ, surrounded by transparent shell and contain coiled tadpole like larvae. Diagnosis is based on detection of adult worms in stool or the eggs in perianal skin.

***Dracunculosis*** is caused by *Dracunculus medinensis*, guinea worm. The disease is endemic to Rajasthan. Female adult worm is long, cord like measuring 60-100 cm, usually found in subcutaneous tissues of leg. Male worm measures only 2-4 cm. The body is cylindrical, smooth and milkywhite in colour. Life span of female worm is 1 year and male worm is 6 months. Embryos are coiled bodies with rounded head and slender tapering tails.

Man is the definitive host and cyclops are the intermediate hosts. Cyclops with larvae are swallowed in drinking water. The larvae penetrate gut wall and in retroperitoneal tissue mature to adult worms. Male dies after fertilization and the gravid female migrates to lower limb to discharge its eggs to exterior.

*Diagnosis* is based on detection of adult worm or its embryo/larvae in smears from discharging sinuses; calcified worms can be seen in X-rays.

***Gnathostomiasis*** in caused by *Gnathostoma spinigerum*, human infection being due to ingestion of larvae in fish, frog or copepods. The larva migrates through intestinal wall to subcutaneous tissues, often visible under the skin being unable to mature. Wandering larva can invade any organ system. Serodiagnosis by immunoblot assay or ELISA are promising.

## Filariasis

Filariasis is caused by *Wuchereria bancrofti* and *Brugia malayi*. The adult worms are found in lymphatic vessels and lymphnodes and the microfilarae in blood. Infection is acquired from bite of culex mosquito containing the infective larva. The infective larva migrate to lymph channel and after 2 moultings mature to adult worm in a year time. After fertilization the gravid female produces the microfilariae that circulate in blood and enter culex mosquito to develop into infective forms.

Diagnosis is from (1) discovery of microfilariae in blood taken between 10 PM-2AM (2) ELISA for filarial antigen (3) demonstration of live worm by US of scrotum/ female breast.

***Oncocerciasis*** (river blindness) is caused by *Oncocerca volvulus*. Man is the definitive host and female black fly, the intermediate host. Incubation period is 1 year. Adult worms live in subcutaneous nodules and release the microfilarae that invade eyes, lymphatics (but not blood).

Diagnosis is based on demonstration of microfilarae in skin snips, in cornea/anterior chamber by slit lamp, and in nodules by ultrasound. Immunoblot analysis and $IgG_4$ antibodies, PCR (on skin snip/urine), antigen detection are dependable.

***Loiasis*** is caused by *Loa loa*. Adult worms live in subcutaneous tissues and release microfilarae into blood stream to be ingested by female chrysops, day biting flies. Fly bite propagates the infection to new host. Diagnosis is by finding the characteristic microfilarae in day time (10Am-4PM) in blood. PCR is also availabe.

***Anisakiasis*** is larval invasion of stomach or intestinal wall by anisakid nematodes, definitive hosts being marine mamnals incliding whales, seals and dolphins. The infective larvae from these mammals pass onto marine fish. Humans contact infection by eating infected marine fish. The larva liberated in intestine cause ulceration, edema and eosinophilic granuloma. Diagnosis is by ELISA and RAST serologic tests.

***Angiostrongyliasis*** is caused by *A. cantonensis* and *A. costaricensis*, manifesting as eosinospilic meningoencephalitis in the former and bowel complications in latter. Human infection in former is due to ingestion of infected larvae in undercooked snails. Diagnosis is based on serologic test and CT/MRI of brain. In latter infection also occurs due to ingestion of undercooked snails, the liberated larvae causing eosinophilic ileocolitis.

***Schistosomiasis*** is caused by *S. haematobium*, *S. mansoni* and *S. japonium*. Humans are main reservoir for former two and mammals for *S. japonicum*. The adult worms live in terminal venules of bladder in *S. haematobium* and of intestim in *S. mansoni and S. japonicum*.The eggs passed in urine and feces reach fresh water, the larvae are released that infect snails - the intermediate host. After development the infective larvae - cercariae leave snail and infect exposed persons through skin and muoues membrane. They reach portal circulation, mature and mate and adult worms reach the venules of intestine and bladder to deposit the eggs.

*S. mansoni* adults live in inferior mesenteric veins of large bowel and *S. japonicum* in superior and inferior mesenteric veins. Egg accumulation in liver can cause periportal fibrosis and portal hypertension. Fibrosis of bladder wall and calcification, ureteral stricture occur in *S. haematobium*.

Diagnosis depends upon detection of eggs of *S. haematobium* in urine and that of *S. japonicum* and *S. mansoni* in stool. 24 hour collected urine be processed and the sediment be examined. Some form of concentration is required to see the eggs in stool. ELISA, immunoblot, CFT, IHA can be used for screening.

***Fasciolopsiasis*** is caused by *Fasciolopsis buski*. Eggs shed in stool reach water and hatch to produce free swimming larvae that penetrate and develop in snails. Cercariae escape from the snails and encyst on various water plants. Humans are infected by cating uncooked water plants (usually chestnuts). The adult parasite 2-7.5 cm long lie in small intestine attached to mucosa, causing gastro intestinal irritation. Diagnosis depends on finding characteristic eggs or occasionally, flukes in stool. No serologic test is available.

***Fascioliasis*** is caused by *Fasciola hepatica*, the sheep liver fluke, resulting from ingestion of encysted metacercariae on watercress or other aquatic vegetables. The metacercariae excyst, penetrate and migrate through the liver and mature in bile ducts. causing hepatomegaly, jaundice, hepatic abscess.

Diagnosis is established by detecting characteristic eggs in feces. US and cholangiography may show the adult parasite in gall bladder and bile duct. ELISA is highly sensitive and specific.

***Clonorchiasis*** is caused by *Clonorchis sinensis* the liver fluke. Eggs shed into water from human/animal feces infect the snails. Larvae escape from snails and encyst in fresh water fish as metacercariae. Human infection results from eating undercooked fish. The ingested parasites excyst in duodenum and ascend the bileducts, where they mature and live for 15-25 years. There is progressive bileduct thickening and fibrosis.

Diagnosis is from characteristic eggs in stool or duodenal aspirate. ELISA is also reliable.

***Paragonimiasis*** is caused by *Paragonimus westermani* the lung fluke. Eggs reach water, either in sputum or feces; hatch, release miracidia that penetrate and develop in snails. Emerging cercariae encyst as metacercariae in the tissues of crabs and crayfish. Human infection is by eating undercooked crustaceans. Metacercariae excyst in small intestine and migrate through diaphragm to settle in lungs forming encysted granulomatous fibrosis. Eggs are discharged from these lesions to be expectorated in sputum. Pulmonary complications include bronchiectasis, bronchopneumonia, lung abscess, fibrosis etc.

*Diagnosis* is made from (1) discovery of characteristic eggs in sputum, pleural fluid, biopsy specimens, CSF (2) ELISA and immunoblot (3) CT scan of chest for fibrotic nodules.

## TAPEWORM INFECTIONS

Six tapeworms infect human beings. The large tape worms are *Taenia saginata* (beef tape worm, upto 25 meter in length); *Taenia solium* (pork tapeworm, upto 7 meter in length), *Diphylobothrium latum* (fish tapeworm, upto 10 m in length); the small tapeworms are *Hymenolepis nana* (dwarf tapeworm– 2.5-4 cm), *Hymenolepis dimunata* (the rodent tape worm, 2-6 cm); and *Dipylidium caninum* (dog tape worm, 1-7 cm). Humans are the only definitive hosts for *T. solium* and *T. saginata*.

An adult tapeworm consists of head (scolex), a neck, and chain of individual segments (proglottids). Eggs form in mature proglottids. Through scolex the worm attaches to intestinal mucosa. Multiple infections are the rule for small tape worms but is rare for larger ones. In beef tape worm, the gravid segments are passed in feces to soil and are ingested by grazing cattle to release the embryos that encyst in muscle as cysticerci (bovis). Human infection occurs by eating undercooked beef. In human intestine the cysticercus develops into an adult worm. The life cycle of pork tape worm is similar except that the pigs ingest the gravid proglottids. Eating under cooked pork containing viable cysticerci (cellulosae) causes human infection. Accidental ingestion of eggs in proglottids contaminating water by humans leads to cysticercosis. Similar is the case if eggs are regurgitated into stomach. In *D. latum* the eggs passed in human feces are taken up by crustaceans that in turn are eaten by fish. Human infection is by eating under cooked fish.

**Tabble 12.1 : Differentiation between T. solium and T. saginata**

| *T. solium* | *T. saginata* |
|---|---|
| 2-3 meter | 5-10 meter |
| < 1000 proglottids | > 1000 proglottids |
| Non pigmented sucker | Pigmented sucker |
| Hooklet present | Absent |
| Rostellum present | Rostellum absent |
| Scolx globular | Scolex quadrate |
| Neck is short | Neck is long |
| Proglottids come out in 5-6 | Single |

*H. nana* is the most common cestode. Its life cycle is unusual in that both larval and adult stage are found in human intestine, internal auto infection can occur and there is no intermediate host. Transmission usually results from eggs transferred directly from human to human. In rodent tapeworm and dog tapeworm infection occurs from accidental ingestion of intermediate hosts like rat fleas or lice.

*Diagnosis* is from discovery of ploglottids in stool, clothing and bedding. To determine the species, proglottid segments are either flattened between glass slides and examined microscopically for anatomic details or differentiated by enzyme electrophoresis of glucose phosphatase isomerase. Perianal cellophane tape test as used to diagnose pin worm can be useful. Detection of taenia specific antigen in stool is also sensitive. Fish tapeworm is diagnosed by finding characteristic operculated eggs is stool. *H. nana* and *H. diminuta* infections are diagnased by finding characteristic eggs in feces; proglottids are not usually seen. *D. caninum* infection is diagnosed by detection of proglottids (the size of melon seeds) in feces. Serological tests are not available for diagnosis of tape worm infections.

**Echinococcosis**

Echinococcosis results from larval stages of 4 echinococcus species – *E. granulosus* (cystic hydatid disease), *E. multilocularis* (alveolar hydatid disease). *E. vogeli* (polycystic hydatid disease) and *E. oligarthrus.* The definitive host is carnivore, usually dog and domestic stock like sheep are intermediate hosts. Human infection occurs when eggs passed in dog feces are accidentally ingested. Liberated embryos penetrate the intestinal mucosa, are carried to liver in portal blood to form hydatid cysts. Larvae can reach lungs to form pulmonary hydatid. The hydatid cystwall has three layers: an inner germinal layer, supporting intermediate layer and an outer layer. Cysts more than 10 cm diameter are usually symptomatic.

Immunoblot test is the test of choice; the arc test is also diagnostic. ELISA, IHA and, immunoflurescence are useful screeting tests. Dead cyst patients are sero negative. US and CT also provide diagnostic clues. Presence of daughter cysts within the cyst are pathognomonic.

The alveolar hydatid cyst has poorly defined borders and behaves like a neoplasm; it infiltrates and proliferates indefinitely by exogenous budding producing an alvelous-like pattern of microvesicles.